A King, and No King

Francis Beaumont and John Fletcher

Contents

A KING, AND NO KING. 7
Persons Represented in the Play..7
Actus primus. Scena prima 8
Actus Secundus 43
Actus Tertius 76
ACTUS QUARTUS 125
Actus Quintus 167
Actus Quinti Scaena Prima..214

A KING, AND NO KING

BY

Francis Beaumont and John Fletcher

A KING, AND NO KING.

By Francis Beaumont and John Fletcher

Persons Represented in the Play.

Arbaces, **King** of Iberia.
Tigranes, **King of** Armenia.
Gobrias, **Lord Protector, and Father of** Arbaces.
Bacurius, *another Lord*.
Mardonius.)
Bessus,) *Two Captains*
Ligo[n]es, **Father of** Spaconia.
Two Gentlemen.
Three Men and a Woman.
Philip, *a servant, and two Citizens Wives*.
A Messenger.
A Servant to Bacurius.
Two Sword-men.
A Boy.
Arane,) The [Queen-Mother.
Panthea,) **Her Daughter**.
Spaconia,) **A Lady Daughter of** Ligones
Mandane,) **A waiting woman, and other attendants**.

Actus primus. Scena prima.

Enter Mardonius *and* Bessus, ***Two Captains***.

Mar.

Bessus, the King has made a fair hand on't, he has ended the
Wars at a blow, would my sword had a close basket hilt to hold
Wine, and the blade would make knives, for we shall have nothing
but eating and drinking.

Bes.

We that are Commanders shall do well enough.

Mar.

Faith ***Bessus***, such Commanders as thou may; I had as lieve set
thee Perdue for a pudding i'th' dark, as ***Alexander*** the Great.

Bes.

I love these jests exceedingly.

Mar.

I think thou lov'st 'em better than quarrelling ***Bessus***, I'le
say so much i'thy behalf, and yet thou 'rt valiant enough upon a
retreat, I think thou wouldst kill any man that stopt thee if

thou couldst.

Bes.

But was not this a brave Combate *Mardonius*?

Mar.

Why, didst thou see't?

Bes.

You stood wi'me.

Mar.

I did so, but me thought thou wink'dst every blow they strook.

Bes.

Well, I believe there are better souldiers than I, that never saw two Princes fight in lists.

Mar.

By my troth I think so too *Bessus*, many a thousand, but certainly all that are worse than thou have seen as much.

Bes.

'Twas bravely done of our King.

Mar.

Yes, if he had not ended the wars: I'me glad thou dar'st talk of such dangerous businesses.

Bes.

To take a Prince prisoner in the heart of's own Country in single combat.

Mar.

See how thy blood curdles at this, I think thou couldst be contented to be beaten i'this passion.

Bes.

Shall I tell you truly?

Mar.

I.

Bes.

I could willingly venture for't.

Mar.

Um, no venture neither *Bessus*.

Bes.

Let me not live, if I do not think 'tis a braver piece of service than that I'me so fam'd for.

Mar.

Why, art thou fam'd for any valour?

Bes.

Fam'd! I, I warrant you.

Mar.

I'me e'en heartily glad on't, I have been with thee e're since thou cam'st to th'wars, and this is the first word that ever I heard on't, prethee who fames thee.

Bes.

The Christian world.

Mar.

'Tis heathenishly done of'em in my conscience, thou deserv'st it not.

Bes.

Yes, I ha' don good service.

Mar.

I do not know how thou mayst wait of a man in's Chamber, or thy agility of shifting of a Trencher, but otherwise no service good *Bessus*.

Bes.

You saw me do the service your self.

Mar.

Not so hasty sweet *Bessus*, where was it, is the place vanish'd?

Bes.

At *Bessus* desp'rate redemption.

Mar.

At *Bessus* desp'rate redemption, where's that?

Bes.

There where I redeem'd the day, the place bears my name.

Mar.

Pray thee, who Christened it?

Bes.

The Souldiers.

Mar.

If I were not a very merrily dispos'd man, what would become of thee? one that had but a grain of choler in the whole composition of his body, would send thee of an errand to the worms for putting thy name upon that field: did not I beat thee there i'th' head o'th' Troops with a Trunchion, because thou wouldst needs run away with thy company, when we should charge the enemy?

Bes.

True, but I did not run.

Mar.

Right *Bessus*, I beat thee out on't.

Bes.

But came I not up when the day was gone, and redeem'd all?

Mar.

Thou knowest, and so do I, thou meanedst to flie, and thy fear making thee mistake, thou ranst upon the enemy, and a hot charge thou gav'st, as I'le do thee right, thou art furious in running away, and I think, we owe thy fear for our victory; If I were the King, and were sure thou wouldst mistake alwaies and run away upon th' enemy, thou shouldst be General by this light.

Bes.

You'l never leave this till I fall foul.

Mar.

No more such words dear *Bessus*, for though I have ever known thee a coward, and therefore durst never strike thee, yet if thou proceedest, I will allow thee valiant, and beat thee.

Bes.

Come, our King's a brave fellow.

Mar.

He is so *Bessus*, I wonder how thou cam'st to know it. But if thou wer't a man of understanding, I would tell thee, he is vain-glorious, and humble, and angry, and patient, and merry and dull, and joyful and sorrowful in extremity in an hour: Do not think me thy friend for this, for if I ear'd who knew it, thou shouldst not hear it *Bessus*. Here he is with his prey in his foot.

Enter &c. Senet Flourish.

Enter Arbaces ***and*** Tigranes, ***Two Kings and two Gentlemen.***

Arb.

Thy sadness brave *Tigranes* takes away
From my full victory, am I become
Of so small fame, that any man should grieve
When I o'recome him? They that plac'd me here,
Intended it an honour large enough, (though he
For the most valiant living, but to dare oppose me single,
Lost the day. What should afflict you, you are as free as I,
To be my prisoner, is to be more free
Than you were formerly, and never think
The man I held worthy to combate me
Shall be us'd servilely: Thy ransom is
To take my only Sister to thy Wife.
A heavy one *Tigranes*, for she is
A Lady, that the neighbour Princes send
Blanks to fetch home. I have been too unkind
To her *Tigranes*, she but nine years old
I left her, and ne're saw her since, your wars
Have held me long and taught me though a youth,
The way to victory, she was a pretty child,
Then I was little better, but now fame
Cries loudly on her, and my messengers
Make me believe she is a miracle;
She'l make you shrink, as I did, with a stroak
But of her eye *Tigranes*.

Tigr.

Is't the course of *Iberia* to use their prisoners thus?
Had fortune thrown my name above *Arbace*,
I should not thus have talk'd Sir, in *Armenia*
We hold it base, you should have kept your temper

Till you saw home again, where 'tis the fashion
Perhaps to brag.

Arb.

Be you my witness earth, need I to brag,
Doth not this captive Prince speak
Me sufficiently, and all the acts
That I have wrought upon his suffering Land;
Should I then boast! where lies that foot of ground
Within his whole Realm, that I have not past,
Fighting and conquering; Far then from me
Be ostentation. I could tell the world
How I have laid his Kingdom desolate
By this sole Arm prop't by divinity,
Stript him out of his glories, and have sent
The pride of all his youth to people graves,
And made his Virgins languish for their Loves,
If I would brag, should I that have the power
To teach the Neighbour world humility,
Mix with vain-glory?

Mar.

Indeed this is none.

Arb.

Tigranes, Nay did I but take delight
To stretch my deeds as others do, on words,
I could amaze my hearers.

Mar.

So you do.

Arb.

But he shall wrong his and my modesty,
That thinks me apt to boast after any act
Fit for a good man to do upon his foe.
A little glory in a souldiers mouth
Is well-becoming, be it far from vain.

Mar.

'Tis pity that valour should be thus drunk.

Arb.

I offer you my Sister, and you answer
I do insult, a Lady that no suite
Nor treasure, nor thy Crown could purchase thee,
But that thou fought'st with me.

Tigr.

Though this be worse
Than that you spake before, it strikes me not;
But that you think to overgrace me with
The marriage of your Sister, troubles me.
I would give worlds for ransoms were they mine,
Rather than have her.

Arb.

See if I insult
That am the Conquerour, and for a ransom
Offer rich treasure to the Conquered,
Which he refuses, and I bear his scorn:
It cannot be self-flattery to say,
The Daughters of your Country set by her,
Would see their shame, run home and blush to death,
At their own foulness; yet she is not fair,
Nor beautiful, those words express her not,
They say her looks have something excellent,
That wants a name: yet were she odious,
Her birth deserves the Empire of the world,
Sister to such a brother, that hath ta'ne
Victory prisoner, and throughout the earth,
Carries her bound, and should he let her loose,
She durst not leave him; Nature did her wrong,
To Print continual conquest on her cheeks,
And make no man worthy for her to taste
But me that am too near her, and as strangely
She did for me, but you will think I brag.

Mar.

I do I'le be sworn. Thy valour and thy passions sever'd, would have made two excellent fellows in their kinds: I know not whether I should be sorry thou art so valiant, or so passionate, wou'd one of 'em were away.

Tigr.

Do I refuse her that I doubt her worth?

Were she as vertuous as she would be thought,
So perfect that no one of her own sex
Could find a want, had she so tempting fair,
That she could wish it off for damning souls,
I would pay any ransom, twenty lives
Rather than meet her married in my bed.
Perhaps I have a love, where I have fixt
Mine eyes not to be mov'd, and she on me,
I am not fickle.

Arb.

Is that all the cause?
Think you, you can so knit your self in love
To any other, that her searching sight
Cannot dissolve it? So before you tri'd,
You thought your self a match for me in [f]ight,
Trust me *Tigranes*, she can do as much
In peace, as I in war, she'l conquer too,
You shall see if you have the power to stand
The force of her swift looks, if you dislike,
I'le send you home with love, and name your ransom
Some other way, but if she be your choice,
She frees you: To *Iberia* you must.

Tigr.

Sir, I have learn'd a prisoners sufferance,
And will obey, but give me leave to talk
In private with some friends before I go.

Arb.

Some to await him forth, and see him safe,
But let him freely send for whom he please,
And none dare to disturb his conference,
I will not have him know what bondage is,

[*Exit Tigranes.*

Till he be free from me. This Prince, *Mardonius*,
Is full of wisdom, valour, all the graces
Man can receive.

Mar.

And yet you conquer'd him.

Arb.

And yet I conquer'd him, and could have don't
Hadst thou joyn'd with him, though thy name in Arms
Be great; must all men that are vertuous
Think suddenly to match themselves with me?
I conquered him and bravely, did I not?

Bes.

And please your Majesty, I was afraid at first.

Mar.

When wert thou other?

Arb.

Of what?

Bes.

That you would not have spy'd your best advantages, for your Majesty in my opinion lay too high, methinks, under favour, you should have lain thus.

Mar.

Like a Taylor at a wake.

Bes.

And then, if please your Majesty to remember, at one time, by my troth I wisht my self wi'you.

Mar.

By my troth thou wouldst ha' stunk 'em both out o'th' Lists.

Arb.

What to do?

Bes.

To put your Majesty in mind of an occasion; you lay thus, and *Tigranes* falsified a blow at your Leg, which you by doing thus avoided; but if you had whip'd up your Leg thus, and reach'd him on the ear, you had made the Blood-Royal run down his head.

Mar.

What Country Fence-school learn'st thou at?

Arb.

Pish, did not I take him nobly?

Mar.

Why you did, and you have talked enough on't.

Arb.

Talkt enough?
Will you confine my word? by heaven and earth,
I were much better be a King of beasts
Than such a people: if I had not patience
Above a God, I should be call'd a Tyrant
Throughout the world. They will offend to death
Each minute: Let me hear thee speak again,
And thou art earth again: why this is like
  Tigranes speech that needs would say I brag'd.
  Bessus, he said I brag'd.

Bes.

Ha, ha, ha.

Arb.

Why dost thou laugh?
By all the world, I'm grown ridiculous

To my own Subjects: Tie me in a Chair
And jest at me, but I shall make a start,
And punish some that others may take heed
How they are haughty; who will answer me?
He said I boasted, speak *Mardonius*,
Did I? He will not answer, O my temper!
I give you thanks above, that taught my heart
Patience, I can endure his silence; what will none
Vouchsafe to give me answer? am I grown
To such a poor respect, or do you mean
To break my wind? Speak, speak, some one of you,
Or else by heaven.

1 Gent.

So please your.

Arb.

Monstrous,
I cannot be heard out, they cut me off,
As if I were too saucy, I will live
In woods, and talk to trees, they will allow me
To end what I begin. The meanest Subject
Can find a freedom to discharge his soul
And not I, now it is a time to speak,
I hearken.

1 Gent.

May it please.

Arb.

I mean not you,
Did not I stop you once? but I am grown
To balk, but I defie, let another speak.

2 Gent.

I hope your Majesty.

Arb.

Thou drawest thy words,
That I must wait an hour, where other men
Can hear in instants; throw your words away,
Quick, and to purpose, I have told you this.

Bes.

And please your Majesty.

Arb.

Wilt thou devour me? this is such a rudeness
As you never shew'd me, and I want
Power to command too, else **Mardonius**
Would speak at my request; were you my King,
I would have answered at your word **Mardonius**,
I pray you speak, and truely, did I boast?

Mar.

Truth will offend you.

Arb.

You take all great care what will offend me,
When you dare to utter such things as these.

Mar.

You told **Tigranes**, you had won his Land,
With that sole arm propt by Divinity:
Was not that bragging, and a wrong to us,
That daily ventured lives?

Arb.

O that thy name
Were as great, as mine, would I had paid my wealth,
It were as great, as I might combate thee,
I would through all the Regions habitable
Search thee, and having found thee, wi'my Sword
Drive thee about the world, till I had met
Some place that yet mans curiosity
Hath mist of; there, there would I strike thee dead:
Forgotten of mankind, such Funeral rites
As beasts would give thee, thou shouldst have.

Bes.

The King rages extreamly, shall we slink away? He'l strike us.

2 Gent.

Content.

Arb.

There I would make you know 'twas this sole arm.
I grant you were my instruments, and did
As I commanded you, but 'twas this arm
Mov'd you like wheels, it mov'd you as it pleas'd.
Whither slip you now? what are you too good
To wait on me (*puffe*,) I had need have temper
That rule such people; I have nothing left
At my own choice, I would I might be private:
Mean men enjoy themselves, but 'tis our curse,
To have a tumult that out of their loves
Will wait on us, whether we will or no;
Go get you gone: Why here they stand like death,
My words move nothing.

1 Gent.

Must we go?

Bes. I know not.

Arb.

I pray you leave me Sirs, I'me proud of this,
That you will be intreated from my sight:
Why now the[y] leave me all: *Mardonius*.

[*Exeunt all but* Arb. *and* Mar.

Mar.

Sir.

Arb.

Will you leave me quite alone? me thinks
Civility should teach you more than this,
If I were but your friend: Stay here and wait.

Mar.

Sir shall I speak?

Arb.

Why, you would now think much
To be denied, but I can scar[c]e intreat
What I would have: do, speak.

Mar.

But will you hear me out?

Arb.

With me you Article to talk thus: well,
I will hear you out.

Mar.

Sir, that I have ever lov'd you, my sword hath spoken for me;
that I do, if it be doubted, I dare call an oath, a great one to

my witness; and were you not my King, from amongst men, I should have chose you out to love above the rest: nor can this challenge thanks, for my own sake I should have done it, because I would have lov'd the most deserving man, for so you are.

Arb.

Alas *Mardonius*, rise you shall not kneel,
We all are souldiers, and all venture lives:
And where there is no difference in mens worths,
Titles are jests, who can outvalue thee?
Mardonius thou hast lov'd me, and hast wrong,
Thy love is not rewarded, but believe
It shall be better, more than friend in arms,
My Father, and my Tutor, good *Mardonius*.

Mar.

Sir, you did promise you would hear me out.

Arb.

And so I will; speak freely, for from thee
Nothing can come but worthy things and true.

Mar.

Though you have all this worth, you hold some qualities that do Eclipse your vertues.

Arb.

Eclipse my vertues?

Mar.

Yes, your passions, which are so manifold, that they appear even
in this: when I commend you, you hug me for that truth: but when
I speak your faults, you make a start, and flie the hearing but.

Arb.

When you commend me? O that I should live
To need such commendations: If my deeds
Blew not my praise themselves about the earth,
I were most wretched: spare your idle praise:
If thou didst mean to flatter, and shouldst utter
Words in my praise, that thou thoughtst impudence,
My deeds should make 'em modest: when you praise I hug
you? 'tis so [false], that wert thou worthy thou shouldst receive
a death, a glorious death from me: but thou shalt understand
thy lies, for shouldst thou praise me into Heaven, and there
leave me inthron'd, I would despise thee though as much as
now, which is as much as dust because I see thy envie.

Mar.

However you will use me after, yet for your own promise sake,
hear me the rest.

Arb.

I will, and after call unto the winds, for they shall lend as
large an ear as I to what you utter: speak.

Mar.

Would you but leave these hasty tempers, which
I do not say take from you all your worth, but darken 'em,
then you will shine indeed.

Arb.

Well.

Mar.

Yet I would have you keep some passions, lest men should take you for a God, your vertues are such.

Arb.

Why now you flatter.

Mar.

I never understood the word, were you no King, and free from these moods, should I choose a companion for wit and pleasure, it should be you; or for honesty to enterchange my bosom with, it should be you; or wisdom to give me counsel, I would pick out you; or valour to defend my reputation, still I should find you out; for you are fit to fight for all the world, if it could come in question: Now I have spoke, consider to your self, find out a use; if so, then what shall fall to me is not material.

Arb.

Is not material? more than ten such lives, as mine, *Mardonius*:

it was nobly said, thou hast spoke truth, and boldly such a truth as might offend another. I have been too passionate and idle, thou shalt see a swift amendment, but I want those parts you praise me for: I fight for all the world? Give me a sword, and thou wilt go as far beyond me, as thou art beyond in years, I know thou dar'st and wilt; it troubles me that I should use so rough a phrase to thee, impute it to my folly, what thou wilt, so thou wilt par[d]on me: that thou and I should differ thus!

Mar.

Why 'tis no matter Sir.

Arb.

Faith but it is, but thou dost ever take all things I do, thus patiently, for which I never can requite thee, but with love, and that thou shalt be sure of. Thou and I have not been merry lately: pray thee tell me where hadst thou that same jewel in thine ear?

Mar.

Why at the taking of a Town.

Arb.

A wench upon my life, a wench **Mardonius** gave thee that jewel.

Mar.

Wench! they respect not me, I'm old and rough, and every limb about me, but that which should, grows stiffer, I'those businesses I may swear I am truly honest: for I pay justly for what I take, and would be glad to be at a certainty.

Arb.

Why, do the wenches encroach upon thee?

Mar.

I by this light do they.

Arb.

Didst thou sit at an old rent with 'em?

Mar.

Yes faith.

Arb.

And do they improve themselves?

Mar.

I ten shillings to me, every new young fellow they come acquainted with.

Arb.

How canst live on't?

Mar.

Why I think I must petition to you.

Arb.

Thou shalt take them up at my price.

Enter two Gentlemen and Bessus.

Mar.

Your price?

Arb.

I at the Kings price.

Mar.

That may be more than I'me worth.

2 Gent.

Is he not merry now?

1 Gent.

I think not.

Bes.

He is, he is: we'l shew our selves.

Arb.

Bessus, I thought you had been in *Iberia* by this, I bad you hast; *Gobrias* will want entertainment for me.

Bes.

And please your Majesty I have a sute.

Arb.

Is't not lousie *Bessus*, what is't?

Bes.

I am to carry a Lady with me.

Arb.

Then thou hast two sutes.

Bes.

And if I can prefer her to the Lady *Pentha* your Majesties Sister, to learn fashions, as her friends term it, it will be worth something to me.

Arb.

So many nights lodgings as 'tis thither, wilt not?

Bes.

I know not that Sir, but gold I shall be sure of.

Arb.

Why thou shalt bid her entertain her from me, so thou wilt resolve me one thing.

Bes.

If I can.

Arb.

Faith 'tis a very disputable question, and yet I think thou canst decide it.

Bes.

Your Majesty has a good opinion of my understanding.

Arb.

I have so good an opinion of it: 'tis whether thou be valiant.

Bes.

Some body has traduced me to you: do you see this sword Sir?

Arb.

Yes.

Bes.

If I do not make my back-biters eat it to a knife within this week, say I am not valiant.

Enter a Messenger.

Mes.

Health to your Majesty.

Arb.

From Gobrias?

Mes.

Yes Sir.

Arb.

How does he, is he well?

Mes.

In perfect health.

Arb.

Take that for thy good news. A trustier servant to his Prince there lives not, than is good Gobrias.

1 Gent.

The King starts back.

Mar.

His blood goes back as fast.

2 Gent. And now it comes again.

Mar.

He alters strangely.

Arb.

The hand of Heaven is on me, be it far from me to struggle, if my secret sins have pull'd this curse upon me, lend me tears now to wash me white, that I may feel a child-like innocence within my breast; which once perform'd, O give me leave to stand as fix'd as constancy her self, my eyes set here unmov'd, regardless of the world though thousand miseries incompass me.

Mar.

This is strange, Sir, how do you?

Arb.

Mardonius, my mother.

Mar.

Is she dead?

Arb.

Alas she's not so happy, thou dost know how she hath laboured since my Father died to take by treason hence this loathed life, that would but be to serve her, I have pardoned, and pardoned, and by that have made her fit to practise new sins, not repent the old: she now had stirr'd a slave to come from thence, and strike me here, whom Gobrias sifting out, took and condemn'd and executed there, the carefulst servant: Heaven let me but live to pay that man; Nature is poor to me, that will not let me have as many deaths as are the times that he hath say'd my life, that I might dye 'em over all for him.

Mar.

Sir let her bear her sins on her own head,
Vex not your self.

Arb.

What will the world
Conceive of me? with what unnatural sins
Will they suppose me loaden, when my life
Is sought by her that gave it to the world?
But yet he writes me comfort here, my Sister,
He saies, is grown in beauty and in grace.
In all the innocent vertues that become
A tender spotless maid: she stains her cheeks
With morning tears to purge her mothers ill,

And 'mongst that sacred dew she mingles Prayers
Her pure Oblations for my safe return:
If I have lost the duty of a Son,
If any pomp or vanity of state
Made me forget my natural offices,
Nay farther, if I have not every night
Expostulated with my wandring thoughts,
If ought unto my parent they have err'd,
And call'd 'em back: do you direct her arm
Unto this foul dissembling heart of mine:
But if I have been just to her, send out
Your power to compass me, and hold me safe
From searching treason; I will use no means
But prayer: for rather suffer me to see
From mine own veins issue a deadly flood,
Than wash my danger off with mothers blood.

Mar.

I n'ere saw such suddain extremities.

[Exeunt.

Enter Tigranes *and* Spaconia.

Tigr.

Why? wilt thou have me die Spaconia.
What should I do?

Spa.

Nay let me stay alone,

And when you see *Armenia* again,
You shall behold a Tomb more worth than I;
Some friend that ever lov'd me or my cause,
Will build me something to distinguish me
From other women, many a weeping verse
He will lay on, and much lament those maids,
That plac'd their loves unfortunately high,
As I have done, where they can never reach;
But why should you go to *Iberia*?

Tigr.

Alas, that thou wilt ask me, ask the man
That rages in a Fever why he lies
Distempered there, when all the other youths
Are coursing o're the Meadows with their Loves?
Can I resist it? am I not a slave
To him that conquer'd me?

Spa.

That conquer'd thee *Tigranes*! he has won
But half of thee, thy body, but thy mind
May be as free as his, his will did never
Combate thine, and take it prisoner.

Tigr.

But if he by force convey my body hence,
What helps it me or thee to be unwilling?

Spa.

O *Tigranes*, I know you are to see a Lady there,
To see, and like I fear: perhaps the hope
Of her make[s] you forget me, ere we part,
Be happier than you know to wish; farewel.

Tigr.

Spaconia, stay and hear me what I say:
In short, destruction meet me that I may
See it, and not avoid it, when I leave
To be thy faithful lover: part with me
Thou shalt not, there are none that know our love,
And I have given gold unto a Captain
That goes unto *Iberia* from the King,
That he will place a Lady of our Land
With the Kings Sister that is offered me;
Thither shall you, and being once got in
Perswade her by what subtil means you can
To be as backward in her love as I.

Spa.

Can you imagine that a longing maid
When she beholds you, can be pull'd away
With words from loving you?

Tigr.

Dispraise my health, my honesty, and tell her I am jealous.

Spa.

Why, I had rather lose you: can my heart
Consent to let my tongue throw out such words,
And I that ever yet spoke what I thought,
Shall find it such a thing at first to lie?

Tigr.

Yet do thy best.

Enter Bessus.

Bes.

What, is your Majesty ready?

Tigr.

There is the Lady, Captain.

Bes.

Sweet Lady, by your leave, I co[u]ld wish my self more full of Courtship for your fair sake.

Spa.

Sir I shall feel no want of that.

Bes.

Lady, you must hast, I have received new letters from the King that require more hast than I expected, he will follow me suddenly himself, and begins to call for your Majesty already.

Tigr.

He shall not do so long.

Bes.

Sweet Lady, shall I call you my Charge hereafter?

Spa.

I will not take upon me to govern your tongue Sir, you shall call me what you please.

Actus Secundus.

Enter Gobrias, Bacurius, Arane, Panthe, *and* Mandane, **Waiting-women with Attendants**.

Gob.

My Lord Bacurius, you must have regard unto the Queen, she is your prisoner, 'tis at your peril if she make escape.

Bac.

My Lord, I know't, she is my prisoner from you committed; yet she is a woman, and so I keep her safe, you will not urge me to keep her close, I shall not shame to say I sorrow for her.

Gob.

So do I my Lord; I sorrow for her, that so little grace doth govern her: that she should stretch her arm against her King, so little womanhood and natural goodness, as to think the death of her own Son.

Ara.

Thou knowst the reason why, dissembling as thou art, and wilt not speak.

Gob.

There is a Lady takes not after you,
Her Father is within her, that good man
Whose tears weigh'd down his sins, mark how she weeps,
How well it does become her, and if you
Can find no disposition in your self
To sorrow, yet by gracefulness in her
Find out the way, and by your reason weep:
All this she does for you, and more she needs
When for your self you will not lose a tear,
Think how this want of grief discredits you,
And you will weep, because you cannot weep.

Ara.

You talk to me as having got a time fit for your purpose; but you should be urg'd know I know you speak not what you think.

Pan.

I would my heart were Stone, before my softness
Against my mother, a more troubled thought
No Virgin bears about; should I excuse
My Mothers fault, I should set light a life
In losing which, a brother and a King
Were taken from me, if I seek to save
That life so lov'd, I lose another life
That gave me being, I shall lose a Mother,
A word of such a sound in a childs ears
That it strikes reverence through it; may the will
Of heaven be done, and if one needs must fall,
Take a poor Virgins life to answer all.

Ara.

But *Gobrias* let us talk, you know this fault
Is not in me as in another Mother.

Gob.

I know it is not.

Ara.

Yet you make it so.

Gob.

Why, is not all that's past beyond your help?

Ara.

I know it is.

Gob.

Nay should you publish it before the world,
Think you 'twould be believ'd?

Ara.

I know it would not.

Gob.

Nay should I joyn with you, should we not both be torn and yet both die uncredited?

Ara.

I think we should.
Gob.

Why then take you such violent courses? As for me I do but right in saving of the King from all your plots.

Ara.

The King?

Gob.

I bad you rest with patience, and a time
Would come for me to reconcile all to
Your own content, but by this way you take
Away my power, and what was done unknown,
Was not by me but you: your urging being done
I must preserve my own, but time may bring
All this to light, and happily for all.

Ara.

Accursed be this over curious brain
That gave that plot a birth, accurst this womb
That after did conceive to my disgrace.

Bac.

My Lord Protector, they say there are divers Letters come from *Armenia*, that *Bessus* has done good service, and brought again a day, by his particular valour, receiv'd you any to that effect?

Gob.

Yes, 'tis most certain.

Bac.

I'm sorry for't, not that the day was won,
But that 'twas won by him: we held him here
A Coward, he did me wrong once, at which I laugh'd,
And so did all the world, for nor I,
Nor any other held him worth my sword.

Enter Bessus ***and*** Spaconia.

Bes.

Health to my Protector; from the King
These Letters; and to your grace Madam, these.

Gob.

How does his Majesty?

Bes.

As well as conquest by his own means and his valiant
C[o]mmanders can make him; your letters will tell you all.

Pan.

I will not open mine till I do know
My Brothers health: good Captain is he well?

Bes.

As the rest of us that fought are.

Pan.

But how's that? is he hurt?

Bes.

He's a strange souldier that gets not a knock.

Pan.

I do not ask how strange that souldier is
That gets no hurt, but whether he have one.

Bes.

He had divers.

Pan.

And is he well again?

Bes.

Well again, an't please your Grace: why I was run twice through the body, and shot i'th' head with a cross-arrow, and yet am well again.

Pan.

I do not care how thou do'st, is he well?

Bes.

Not care how I do? Let a man out of the mightiness of his spirit, fructifie Foreign Countries with his blood for the good of his own, and thus he shall be answered: Why I may live to relieve with spear and shield, such a Lady as you distressed.

Pan.

Why, I will care, I'me glad that thou art well, I prethee is he so?

Gob.

The King is well and will be here to morrow.

Pan.

My prayer is heard, now will I open mine.

Gob.

Bacurius, I must ease you of your charge:
Madam, the wonted mercy of the King,
That overtakes your faults, has met with this,
And struck it out, he has forgiven you freely,
Your own will is your law, be where you please.

Ara.

I thank him.

Gob.

You will be ready to wait upon his Majesty to morrow?

Ara.

I will.

[*Exit* Arane.

Bac.

Madam be wise hereafter; I am glad I have lost this Office.

Gob.

Good Captain **Bessus**, tell us the discourse betwixt **Tigranes** and our King, and how we got the victory.

Pan.

I prethee do, and if my Brother were
In any danger, let not thy tale make
Him abide there long before thou bring him off,
For all that while my heart will beat.

Bes.

Madam let what will beat, I must tell the truth, and thus it was; they fought single in lists, but one to one; as for my own part, I was dangerously hurt but three days before, else, perhaps, we had been two to two, I cannot tell, some thought we had, and the occasion of my hurt was this, the enemy had made Trenches.

Gob.

Captain, without the manner of your hurt be much material to this business, we'l hear't some other time.

Pan.

I prethee leave it, and go on with my Brother.

Bes.

I will, but 'twould be worth your hearing: To the
Lists they came, and single-sword and gantlet was their fight.

Pan.

Alas!

Bes.

Without the Lists there stood some dozen Captains of either side
mingled, all which were sworn, and one of those was I: and 'twas
my chance to stand next a Captain o'th' enemies side, called
Tiribasus; Valiant they said he was; whilst these two Kings
were streaching themselves, this ***Tiribasus*** cast something a
scornful look on me, and ask't me who I thought would overcome: I
smil'd and told him if he would fight with me, he should perceive
by the event of that whose King would win: something he answered,
and a scuffle was like to grow, when one ***Zipetus*** offered to
help him, I--

Pan.

All this is of thy self, I pray thee ***Bessus*** tell something of
my Brother, did he nothing?

Bes.

Why yes, I'le tell your Grace, they were not to fight till the
word given, which for my own part, by my troth I confess I was
not to give.

Pan.

See for his own part.

Bac.

I fear yet this fellow's abus'd with a good report.

Bes.

But I--

Pan.

Still of himself.

Bes.

Cri'd give the word, when as some of them say, *Tigranes* was stooping, but the word was not given then, yet one *Cosroes* of the enemies part, held up his finger to me, which is as much with us Martialists, as I will fight with you: I said not a word, nor made sign during the combate, but that once done.

Pan.

He slips o're all the fight.

Bes.

I call'd him to me, *Cosroes* said I.

Pan.

I will hear no more.

Bes.

No, no, I lie.

Bac.

I dare be sworn thou dost.

Bes.

Captain said I, so it was.

Pan.

I tell thee, I will hear no further.

Bes.

No? Your Grace will wish you had.

Pan.

I will not wish it, what is this the Lady
My brother writes to me to take?

Bes.

And please your Grace this is she: Charge, will you come near the

Princess?

Pan.

You'r welcome from your Country, and this land shall shew unto you all the kindness that I can make it; what's your name?

Spa.

Thalectris.

Pan.

Y'are very welcome, you have got a letter to put you to me, that has power enough to place mine enemy here; then much more you that are so far from being so to me that you ne're saw me.

Bes.

Madam, I dare pass my word for her truth.

Spa.

My truth?

Pan.

Why Captain, do you think I am afraid she'l steal?

Bes.

I cannot tell, servants are slippery, but I dare give my word for her, and for honesty, she came along with me, and many favours she did me by the way, but by this light none but what she might do with modesty, to a man of my rank.

Pan.

Why Captain, here's no body thinks otherwise.

Bes.

Nay, if you should, your Grace may think your pleasure; but I am sure I brought her from *Armenia*, and in all that way, if ever I touch'd any bare of her above her knee, I pray God I may sink where I stand.

Spa.

Above my knee?

Bes.

No, you know I did not, and if any man will say, I did, this sword shall answer; Nay, I'le defend the reputation of my charge whilst I live, your Grace shall understand I am secret in these businesses, and know how to defend a Ladies honour.

Spa.

I hope your Grace knows him so well already, I shall not need to tell you he's vain and foolish.

Bes.

I you may call me what you please, but I'le defend your good name against the world; and so I take my leave of your Grace, and of you my Lord Protector; I am likewise glad to see your Lordship well.

Bac.

O Captain *Bessus*, I thank you, I would speak with you anon.

Bes.

When you please, I will attend your Lordship.

Bac.

Madam, I'le take my leave too.

Pan.

Good *Bacurius*.

[*Exeunt* Bes. *and* Bac.

Gob.

Madam what writes his Majesty to you?

Pan.

O my Lord, the kindest words, I'le keep 'em whilst I live, here in my bosom, there's no art in 'em, they lie disordered in this paper, just as hearty nature speaks 'em.

Gob.

And to me he writes what tears of joy he shed to hear how you were grown in every vertues way, and yields all thanks to me, for that dear care which I was bound to have in training you, there is no Princess living that enjoys a brother of that worth.

Pan.

My Lord, no maid longs more for any thing,
And feels more heat and cold within her breast,
Than I do now, in hopes to see him.

Gob.

Yet I wonder much
At this he writes, he brings along with him
A husband for you, that same Captive Prince,
And if he loves you as he makes a shew,
He will allow you freedom in your choice.

Pan.

And so he will my Lord, I warrant you, he will but offer and give me the power to take or leave.

Gob.

Trust me, were I a Lady, I could not like that man were bargain'd with before I choose him.

Pan.

But I am not built on such wild humours, if I find him worthy, he is not less because he's offer'd.

Spa.

'Tis true, he is not, would he would seem less.

Gob.

I think there's no Lady can affect
Another Prince, your brother standing by;
He doth Eclipse mens vertues so with his.

Spa.

I know a Lady may, and more I fear
Another Lady will.

Pan.

Would I might see him.

Gob.

Why so you shall, my businesses are great,
I will attend you when it is his pleasure to see you.

Pan.

I thank you good my Lord.

Gob.

You will be ready Madam.

[Exit Gob.

Pan.

Yes.

Spa.

I do beseech you Madam, send away
Your other women, and receive from me
A few sad words, which set against your joyes
May make 'em shine the more.

Pan.

Sirs, leave me all.

[Exeunt Women.

Spa.

I kneel a stranger here to beg a thing
Unfit for me to ask, and you to grant,
'Tis such another strange ill-laid request,
As if a begger should intreat a King
To leave his Scepter, and his Throne to him
And take his rags to wander o're the world
Hungry and cold.

Pan.

That were a strange request.

Spa.

As ill is mine.

Pan. Then do not utter it.

Spa.

Alas 'tis of that nature, that it must
Be utter'd, I, and granted, or I die:
I am asham'd to speak it; but where life
Lies at the stake, I cannot think her woman

That will not take something unreasonably to hazard saving of it:
I shall seem a strange Petitioner, that wish all ill to them I
beg of, e're they give me ought; yet so I must: I would you were
not fair, nor wise, for in your ill consists my good: if you were
foolish, you would hear my prayer, if foul, you had not power to
hinder me: he would not love you.

Pan.

What's the meaning of it.

Spa.

Nay, my request is more without the bounds
Of reason yet: for 'tis not in the power
Of you to do, what I would have you grant.

Pan.

Why then 'tis idle, pray thee speak it out.
Spa.

Your brother brings a Prince into this land,
Of such a noble shape, so sweet a grace,
So full of worth withal, that every maid
That looks upon him, gives away her self
To him for ever; and for you to have
He brings him: and so mad is my demand
That I desire you not to have this man,
This excellent man, for whom you needs must die,
If you should miss him. I do now expect
You should laugh at me.

Pan.

Trust me I could weep rather, for I have found him
In all thy words a strange disjoynted sorrow.

Spa.

'Tis by me his own desire so, that you would not love him.

Pan.

His own desire! why credit me *Thalestris,* I am no common wooer:
if he shall wooe me, his worth may be such, that I dare not swear
I will not love him; but if he will stay to have me wooe him, I
will promise thee, he may keep all his graces to himself, and
fear no ravishing from me.

Spa.

'Tis yet his own desire, but when he sees your face, I fear it
will not be; therefore I charge you as you have pity, stop these
tender ears from his enchanting voice, close up those eyes, that
you may neither catch a dart from him, nor he from you; I charge
you as you hope to live in quiet; for when I am dead, for certain
I will walk to visit him if he break promise with me: for as fast
as Oaths without a formal Ceremony can make me, I am to him.

Pan.

Then be fearless;
For if he were a thing 'twixt God and man,
I could gaze on him; if I knew it sin
To love him without passion: Dry your eyes,
I swear you shall enjoy him still for me,
I will not hinder you; but I perceive
You are not what you seem, rise, rise *Thalestris*,
If your right name be so.

Spa.

Indeed it is not, *Spaconia* is my name; but I desire not to be
known to other.

Pan.

Why, by me you shall not, I will never do you wrong, what good I
can, I will, think not my birth or education such, that I should
injure a stranger Virgin; you are welcome hither, in company you
wish to be commanded, but when we are alone, I shall be ready to
be your servant.

[*Exeunt*.

Enter three Men and a Woman.

1.

Come, come, run, run, run.

2.

We shall out-go her.

3.

One were better be hang'd than carry out women fidling to these shews.

Wom.

Is the King hard by?

1.

You heard he with the Bottles said, he thought we should come too late: What abundance of people here is!

Wom.

But what had he in those Bottles?

3.

I know not.

2.

Why, Ink goodman fool.

3.

Ink, what to do?

1.

Why the King look you, will many times call for these Bottles, and break his mind to his friends.

Wom.

Let's take our places, we shall have no room else.

2.

The man told us he would walk o' foot through the people.

3.

I marry did he.

1.

Our shops are well look't to now.

2.

'Slife, yonder's my Master, I think.

1.

No 'tis not he.

Enter a man with two Citizens-wives.

1 Cit.

Lord how fine the fields be, what sweet living 'tis in the Country!

2 Cit.

I poor souls, God help 'em; they live as contentedly as one of us.

1 Cit.

My husbands Cousin would have had me gone into the Country last year, wert thou ever there?

2 Cit.

I, poor souls, I was amongst 'em once.

1 Cit.

And what kind of creatures are they, for love of God?

2 Cit.

Very good people, God help 'em.

1 Cit.

Wilt thou go down with me this Summer when I am brought to bed?

2 Cit.

Alas, it is no place for us.

1 Cit.

Why, pray thee?

2 Cit.

Why you can have nothing there, there's no body cryes brooms.

1 Cit.

No?

2 Cit.

No truly, nor milk.

1 Cit.

Nor milk, how do they?

2 Cit.

They are fain to milk themselves i'th' Country.

1 Cit.

Good Lord! but the people there, I think, will be very dutiful to one of us.

2 Cit.

I God knows will they, and yet they do not greatly care for our husbands.

1 Cit.

Do they not? Alas! I'good faith I cannot blame them: for we do not greatly care for them our selves. ***Philip***, I pray choose us a place.

Phil.

There's the best forsooth.

1 Cit.

By your leave good people a little.

3.

What's the matter?

Phil.

I pray you my friend, do not thrust my Mistress so, she's with

Child.

2.

Let her look to her self then, has she not had showing enough yet? if she stay shouldring here, she may haps go home with a cake in her belly.

3.

How now, goodman squitter-breech, why do you lean on me?

Phi.

Because I will.

3.

Will you Sir sawce-box?

1 Cit.

Look if one ha'not struck *Philip*, come hither *Philip*, why did he strike thee?

Phil.

For leaning on him.

1 Cit.

Why didst thou lean on him?

***Phil*.**

I did not think he would have struck me.

***1 Cit*.**

As God save me la thou'rt as wild as a Buck, there's no quarel but thou'rt at one end or other on't.

***3*.**

It's at the first end then, for he'l ne'r stay the last.

***1 Cit*.**

Well slip-string, I shall meet with you.

***3*.**

When you will.

***1 Cit*.**

I'le give a crown to meet with you.

***3*.**

At a Bawdy-house.

***1 Cit*.**

I you're full of your Roguery; but if I do meet you it shall cost me a fall.

Flourish. Enter one running.

4

The King, the King, the King. Now, now, now, now.

Flourish. Enter Arb. Tigr. ***The two Kings and*** Mardonius.

All.

God preserve your Majesty.

Arb.

I thank you all, now are my joyes at full, when I behold you safe, my loving Subjects; by you I grow, 'tis your united love that lifts me to this height: all the account that I can render you for all the love you have bestowed on me, all your expences to maintain my war, is but a little word, you will imagine 'tis slender paiment, yet 'tis such a word, as is not to be bought but with your bloods, 'tis Peace.

All.

God preserve your Majesty.

Arb.

Now you may live securely i'your Towns,
Your Children round about you; may sit
Under your Vines, and make the miseries

Of other Kingdoms a discourse for you,
And lend them sorrows; for your selves, you may
Safely forget there are such things as tears,
And you may all whose good thoughts I have gain'd,
Hold me unworthy, where I think my life
A sacrifice too great to keep you thus
In such a calm estate.

All.

God bless your Majesty.

Arb.

See all good people, I have brought the man whose very name you fear'd, a captive home; behold him, 'tis ***Tigranes***; in your heart sing songs of gladness, and deliverance.

1 Cit.

Out upon him.

2 Cit.

How he looks.

3 Wom.

Hang him, hang him.

Mar.

These are sweet people.

Tigr.

Sir, you do me wrong, to render me a scorned spectacle to common people.

Arb.

It was so far from me to mean it so: if I have ought deserv'd, my loving Subjects, let me beg of you, not to revile this Prince, in whom there dwells all worth of which the name of a man is capable, valour beyond compare, the terrour of his name has stretcht it self where ever there is sun; and yet for you I fought with him single, and won him too; I made his valour stoop, and brought that name soar'd to so unbeliev'd a height, to fall beneath mine: this inspir'd with all your loves, I did perform, and will for your content, be ever ready for a greater work.

All.

The Lord bless your Majesty.

Tigr.

So he has made me amends now with a speech in commendation of himself: I would not be so vain-glorious.

Arb.

If there be any thing in which I may
Do good to any creature, here speak out;
For I must leave you: and it troubles me,

That my occasions for the good of you,
Are such as call me from you: else, my joy
Would be to spend my days among you all.
You shew your loves in these large multitudes
That come to meet me, I will pray for you,
Heaven prosper you, that you may know old years,
And live to see your childrens children sit
At your boards with plenty: when there is
A want of any thing, let it be known
To me, and I will be a Father to you:
God keep you all.

[*Flourish. Exeunt Kings and their Train*.

All.

God bless your Majesty, God bless your Majesty.

1.

Come, shall we go? all's done.

Wom.

I for God sake, I have not made a fire yet.

2.

Away, away, all's done.

3.

Content, farewel *Philip*.

1 Cit.

Away you halter-sack you.

2.

Philip will not fight, he's afraid on's face.

Phil.

I marry am I afraid of my face.

3.

Thou wouldst be *Philip* if thou sawst it in a glass; it looks so like a Visour.

[*Exeunt 2., 3., and Woman*.

1 Cit.

You'l be hang'd sirra: Come *Philip* walk before us homewards; did not his Majesty say he had brought us home Pease for all our money?

2 Cit.

Yes marry did he.

1 Cit.

They're the first I heard of this year by my troth, I longed for some of 'em: did he not say we should have some?

2 Cit.

Yes, and so we shall anon I warrant you have every one a peck brought home to our houses.

Actus Tertius.

Enter Arbaces *and* Gobrias.

Arb.

My Sister take it ill?

Gob.

Not very ill.
Something unkindly she does take it Sir to have
Her Husband chosen to her hands.

Arb.

Why *Gobrias* let her, I must have her know, my will and not her own must govern her: what will she marry with some slave at home?

Gob.

O she is far from any stubbornness, you much mistake her, and no doubt will like where you would have her, but when you behold her, you will be loth to part with such a jewel.

Arb.

To part with her? why *Gobrias*, art thou mad? she is my Sister.

Gob.

Sir, I know she is: but it were pity to make poor our Land, with such a beauty to enrich another.

Arb.

Pish will she have him?

Gob.

I do hope she will not, I think she will Sir.

Arb.

Were she my Father and my Mother too, and all the names for which we think folks friends, she should be forc't to have him when I know 'tis fit: I will not hear her say she's loth.

Gob.

Heaven bring my purpose luckily to pass, you know 'tis just, she will not need constraint she loves you so.

Arb.

How does she love me, speak?

Gob.

She loves you more than people love their health,
that live by labour; more than I could love a man that died
for me, if he could live again.

Arb.

She is not like her mother then.

Gob.

O no, when you were in *Armenia*,
I durst not let her know when you were hurt:
For at the first on every little scratch,
She kept her Chamber, wept, and could not eat,
Till you were well, and many times the news
Was so long coming, that before we heard
She was as near her death, as you your health.

Arb.

Alas poor soul, but yet she must be rul'd;
I know not how I shall requite her well.
I long to see her, have you sent for her,
To tell her I am ready?

Gob.

Sir I have.

Enter 1 Gent, *and* Tigranes.

1 Gent.

Sir, here is the *Armenian* King.

Arb.

He's welcome.

1 Gent.

And the Queen-mother, and the Princess wait without.

Arb.

Good *Gobrias* bring 'em in.
Tigranes, you will think you are arriv'd
In a strange Land, where Mothers cast to poyson
Their only Sons; think you you shall be safe?

Tigr.

Too safe I am Sir.

Enter Gobrias, Arane, Panthea, Spaconia, Bacurius, Mardonius *and* Bessus, **and two Gentlemen**.

Ara.

As low as this I bow to you, and would
As low as is my grave, to shew a mind
Thankful for all your mercies.

Arb.

O stand up,
And let me kneel, the light will be asham'd
To see observance done to me by you.

Ara.

You are my King.

Arb.

You are my Mother, rise;
As far be all your faults from your own soul,
As from my memory; then you shall be
As white as innocence her self.

Ara.

I came
Only to shew my duty, and acknowledge
My sorrows for my sins; longer to stay
Were but to draw eyes more attentively
Upon my shame, that power that kept you safe

From me, preserve you still.

Arb.

Your own desires shall be your guide.

[*Exit* Arane.

Pan.

Now let me die, since I have seen my Lord the King
Return in safetie, I have seen all good that life
Can shew me; I have ne're another wish
For Heaven to grant, nor were it fit I should;
For I am bound to spend my age to come,
In giving thanks that this was granted me.

Gob.

Why does not your Majesty speak?

Arb.

To whom?

Gob.

To the Princess.

Pan.

Alas Sir, I am fearful, you do look

On me, as if I were some loathed thing
That you were finding out a way to shun.

***Gob*.**

Sir, you should speak to her.

***Arb*.**

Ha?

***Pan*.**

I know I am unworthy, yet not ill arm'd, with which innocence here I will kneel, till I am one with earth, but I will gain some words and kindness from you.

***Tigr*.**

Will you speak Sir?

***Arb*.**

Speak, am I what I was?
What art thou that dost creep into my breast,
And dar'st not see my face? shew forth thy self:
I feel a pair of fiery wings displai'd
Hither, from hence; you shall not tarry there,
Up, and be gone, if thou beest Love be gone:
Or I will tear thee from my wounded breast,
Pull thy lov'd Down away, and with thy Quill
By this right arm drawn from thy wonted wing,
Write to thy laughing Mother i'thy bloud,

That you are powers bely'd, and all your darts
Are to be blown away, by men resolv'd,
Like dust; I know thou fear'st my words, away.
Tigr.

O misery! why should he be so slow?
There can no falshood come of loving her;
Though I have given my faith; she is a thing
Both to be lov'd and serv'd beyond my faith:
I would he would present me to her quickly.

Pan.

Will you not speak at all? are you so far
From kind words? yet to save my modesty,
That must talk till you answer, do not stand
As you were dumb, say something, though it be
Poyson'd with anger, that it may strike me dead.

Mar.

Have you no life at all? for man-hood sake
Let her not kneel, and talk neglected thus;
A tree would find a tongue to answer her,
Did she but give it such a lov'd respect.

Arb.

You mean this Lady: lift her from the earth; why do you let her
kneel so long? Alas, Madam, your beauty uses to command, and not
to beg. What is your sute to me? it shall be granted, yet the
time is short, and my affairs are great: but where's my Sister? I
bade she should be brought.

Mar.

What, is he mad?

Arb.

Gobrias, where is she?

Gob.

Sir.

Arb.

Where is she man?

Gob.

Who, Sir?

Arb.

Who, hast thou forgot my Sister?

Gob.

Your Sister, Sir?

Arb.

Your Sister, Sir? some one that hath a wit, answer, where is she?

Gob.

Do you not see her there?

Arb.

Where?

Gob.

There.

Arb.

There, where?

Mar.

S'light, there, are you blind?

Arb.

Which do you mean, that little one?

Gob.

No Sir.

Arb.

No Sir? why, do you mock me? I can see
No other here, but that petitioning Lady.

Gob.

That's she.

Arb.

Away.

Gob.

Sir, it is she.

Arb.

'Tis false.

Gob.

Is it?

Arb.

As hell, by Heaven, as false as hell,
My Sister: is she dead? if it be so,
Speak boldly to me; for I am a man,
And dare not quarrel with Divinity;
And do not think to cozen me with this:
I see you all are mute and stand amaz'd,
Fearful to answer me; it is too true,
A decreed instant cuts off ev'ry life,

For which to mourn, is to repine; she dy'd
A Virgin, though more innocent than sheep,
As clear as her own eyes, and blessedness
Eternal waits upon her where she is:
I know she could not make a wish to change
Her state for new, and you shall see me bear
My crosses like a man; we all must die,
And she hath taught us how.

Gob.

Do not mistake,
And vex your self for nothing; for her death
Is a long life off, I hope: 'Tis she,
And if my speech deserve not faith, lay death
Upon me, and my latest words shall force
A credit from you.

Arb.

Which, good Gobrias? that Lady dost thou mean?

Gob.

That Lady Sir,
She is your Sister, and she is your Sister
That loves you so, 'tis she for whom I weep,
To see you use her thus.

Arb.

It cannot be.

Tigr.

Pish, this is tedious,
I cannot hold, I must present my self,
And yet the sight of my *Spaconia*
Touches me, as a sudden thunder-clap
Does one that is about to sin.

Arb.

Away,
No more of this; here I pronounce him Traytor,
The direct plotter of my death, that names
Or thinks her for my Sister, 'tis a lie,
The most malicious of the world, invented
To mad your King; he that will say so next,
Let him draw out his sword and sheath it here,
It is a sin fully as pardonable:
She is no kin to me, nor shall she be;
If she were ever, I create her none:
And which of you can question this? My power
Is like the Sea, that is to be obey'd,
And not disputed with: I have decreed her
As far from having part of blood with me,
As the nak'd *indians*; come and answer me,
He that is boldest now; is that my Sister?

Mar.

O this is fine.

Bes.

No marry, she is not, an't please your Majesty,
I never thought she was, she's nothing like you.

Arb.

No 'tis true, she is not.

Mar.

Thou shou'dst be hang'd.

Pan.

Sir, I will speak but once; by the same power
You make my blood a stranger unto yours,
You may command me dead, and so much love
A stranger may importune, pray you do;
If this request appear too much to grant,
Adopt me of some other Family,
By your unquestion'd word; else I shall live
Like sinfull issues that are left in streets
By their regardless Mothers, and no name
Will be found for me.

Arb.

I will hear no more,
Why should there be such musick in a voyce,
And sin for me to hear it? All the world
May take delight in this, and 'tis damnation
For me to do so: You are fair and wise
And vertuous I think, and he is blest
That is so near you as my brother is;

But you are nought to me but a disease;
Continual torment without hope of ease;
Such an ungodly sickness I have got,
That he that undertakes my cure, must first
O'rethrow Divinity, all moral Laws,
And leave mankind as unconfin'd as beasts,
Allowing 'em to do all actions
As freely as they drink when they desire.
Let me not hear you speak again; yet see
I shall but lang[u]ish for the want of that,
The having which, would kill me: No man here
Offer to speak for her; for I consider
As much as you can say; I will not toil
My body and my mind too, rest thou there,
Here's one within will labour for you both.

Pan.

I would I were past speaking.

Gob.

Fear not Madam,
The King will alter, 'tis some sudden rage,
And you shall see it end some other way.

Pan.

Pray heaven it do.

Tig.

Though she to whom I swore, be here, I cannot

Stifle my passion longer; if my father
Should rise again disquieted with this,
And charge me to forbear, yet it would out.
Madam, a stranger, and a pris'ner begs
To be bid welcome.

Pan.

You are welcome, Sir,
I think, but if you be not, 'tis past me
To make you so: for I am here a stranger,
Greater than you; we know from whence you come,
But I appear a lost thing, and by whom
Is yet uncertain, found here i'th' Court,
And onely suffer'd to walk up and down,
As one not worth the owning.

Spa.

O, I fear
Tigranes will be caught, he looks, me-thinks,
As he would change his eyes with her; some help
There is above for me, I hope.

Tigr.

Why do you turn away, and weep so fast,
And utter things that mis-become your looks,
Can you want owning?

Spa.

O 'tis certain so.

Tigr.

Acknowledge your self mine.

Arb.

How now?

Tigr.

And then see if you want an owner.

Arb.

They are talking.

Tigr.

Nations shall owne you for their Queen.

Arb.

Tigranes, art not thou my prisoner?

Tigr.

I am.

Arb.

And who is this?

Tigr.

She is your Sister.

Arb.

She is so.

Mar.

Is she so again? that's well.

Arb.

And then how dare you offer to change words with her?

Tigr.

Dare do it! Why? you brought me hither Sir,
To that intent.

Arb.

Perhaps I told you so,
If I had sworn it, had you so much folly
To credit it? The least word that she speaks
Is worth a life; rule your disordered tongue,
Or I will temper it.

Spa.

Blest be the breath.

Tigr.

Temper my tongue! such incivilities
As these, no barbarous people ever knew:
You break the lawes of Nature, and of Nations,
You talk to me as if I were a prisoner
For theft: my tongue be temper'd? I must speak
If thunder check me, and I will.

Arb.

You will?

Spa.

Alas my fortune.

Tigr.

Do not fear his frown, dear Madam, hear me.

Arb.

Fear not my frown? but that 'twere base in me
To fight with one I know I can o'recome,
Again thou shouldst be conquer'd by me.

Mar.

He has one ransome with him already; me-thinks

'T were good to fight double, or quit.

Arb.

Away with him to prison: Now Sir, see
If my frown be regardless; Why delay you?
Seise him *Bacurius*, you shall know my word
Sweeps like a wind, and all it grapples with,
Are as the chaffe before it.

Tigr.

Touch me not.

Arb.

Help there.

Tigr.

Away.

1 Gent.

It is in vain to struggle.

2 Gent.

You must be forc'd.

Bac.

Sir, you must pardon us, we must obey.

Arb.

Why do you dally there? drag him away
By any thing.

Bac.

Come Sir.

Tigr.

Justice, thou ought'st to give me strength enough
To shake all these off; This is tyrannie,
Arbaces, sutler than the burning Bulls,
Or that fam'd *Titans* bed. Thou mightst as well
Search i'th' deep of Winter through the snow
For half starv'd people, to bring home with thee,
To shew 'em fire, and send 'em back again,
As use me thus.

Arb.

Let him be close, *Bacurius*.

[*Exeunt* Tigr. *And* Bac.

Spa.

I ne're rejoyc'd at any ill to him,
But this imprisonment: what shall become

Of me forsaken?

***Gob*.**

You will not let your Sister
Depart thus discontented from you, Sir?

***Arb*.**

By no means ***Gobrias***, I have done her wrong,
And made my self believe much of my self,
That is not in me: You did kneel to me,
Whilest I stood stubborn and regardless by,
And like a god incensed, gave no ear
To all your prayers: behold, I kneel to you,
Shew a contempt as large as was my own,
And I will suffer it, yet at the last forgive me.

***Pan*.**

O you wrong me more in this,
Than in your rage you did: you mock me now.

***Arb*.**

Never forgive me then, which is the worst
Can happen to me.

***Pan*.**

If you be in earnest,
Stand up and give me but a gentle look,

And two kind words, and I shall be in heaven.

Arb.

Rise you then to hear; I acknowledge thee
My hope, the only jewel of my life,
The best of Sisters, dearer than my breath,
A happiness as high as I could think;
And when my actions call thee otherwise,
Perdition light upon me.

Pan.

This is better
Than if you had not frown'd, it comes to me,
Like mercie at the block, and when I leave
To serve you with my life, your curse be with me.

Arb.

Then thus I do salute thee, and again,
To make this knot the stronger, Paradise
Is there: It may be you are yet in doubt,
This third kiss blots it out, I wade in sin,
And foolishly intice my self along;
Take her away, see her a prisoner
In her own chamber closely, *Gobrias*.

Pan.

Alas Sir, why?

Arb.

I must not stay the answer, doe it.

Gob.

Good Sir.

Arb.

No more, doe it I say.

Mard.

This is better and better.

Pan.

Yet hear me speak.

Arb.

I will not hear you speak,
Away with her, let no man think to speak
For such a creature; for she is a witch,
A prisoner, and a Traitor.

Gob.

Madam, this office grieves me.

Pan.

Nay, 'tis well the king is pleased with it.

Arb.

Bessus, go you along too with her; I will prove
All this that I have said, if I may live
So long; but I am desperately sick,
For she has given me poison in a kiss;
She had't betwixt her lips, and with her eyes
She witches people: go without a word.

[*Exeunt* Gob. Pan. Bes. *And* Spaconia.

Why should you that have made me stand in war
Like fate it self, cutting what threds I pleas'd,
Decree such an unworthy end of me,
And all my glories? What am I, alas,
That you oppose me? if my secret thoughts
Have ever harbour'd swellings against you,
They could not hurt you, and it is in you
To give me sorrow, that will render me
Apt to receive your mercy; rather so,
Let it be rather so, than punish me
With such unmanly sins: Incest is in me
Dwelling already, and it must be holy
That pulls it thence, where art *Mardonius*?

Mar.

Here Sir.

Arb.

I pray thee bear me, if thou canst,
Am I not grown a strange weight?

Mar.

As you were.

Arb.

No heavier?

Mar.

No Sir.

Arb.

Why, my legs
Refuse to bear my body; O *Mardonius*,
Thou hast in field beheld me, when thou knowst
I could have gone, though I could never run.

Mar.

And so I shall again.

Arb.

O no, 'tis past.

Mar.

Pray you go rest your self.

Arb.

Wilt thou hereafter when they talk of me,
As thou shalt hear nothing but infamy,
Remember some of those things?

Mar.

Yes I will.

Arb.

I pray thee do: for thou shalt never see me so again.

[*Exeunt.*

Enter Bessus alone.

Bes.

They talk of fame, I have gotten it in the wars; and will afford any man a reasonable penny-worth: some will say, they could be content to have it, but that it is to be atchiev'd with danger; but my opinion is otherwise: for if I might stand still in Cannon-proof, and have fame fall upon me, I would refuse it: my reputation came principally by thinking to run away, which no body knows but *Mardonius*, and I think he conceals it to anger me. Before I went to the warrs, I came to the Town a young fellow, without means or parts to deserve friends; and my empty guts perswaded me to lie, and abuse people for my meat, which I did, and they beat me: then would I fast two days, till my hunger cri'd out on me, rail still, then me-thought I had a monstrous stomach to abuse 'em again, and did it. I, this state I continu'd till they hung me up by th' heels, and beat me wi' hasle sticks, as if they would have baked me, and have cousen'd some body wi'me for Venison: After this I rail'd, and eat quietly: for the whole Kingdom took notice of me for a baffl'd whipt fellow, and what I said was remembred in mirth but never in anger, of which I was glad; I would it were at that pass again. After this, heaven calls an Aunt of mine, that left two hundred pound in a cousins hand for me, who taking me to be a gallant young spirit, raised a company for me with the money and sent me into *Armenia* with 'em: Away I would have run from them, but that I could get no company, and alone I durst not run. I was never at battail but once, and there I was running, but *Mardonius* cudgel'd me; yet I got loose at last, but was so fraid, that I saw no more than my shoulders doe, but fled with my whole company amongst my Enemies, and overthrew 'em: Now the report of my valour is come over before me, and they say I was a raw young fellow, but now I am improv'd, a Plague on their eloquence, 't will cost me many a beating; And *Mardonius* might help this too, if he would; for now they think to get honour on me, and all the men I have abus'd call me freshly worthily, as they call it by the way of challenge.

Enter a Gent.

3 Gent.

Good morrow, Captain *Bessus*.

Bes.

Good morrow Sir.

3 Gent.

I come to speak with you.

Bes.

You're very welcome.

3 Gent.

From one that holds himself wrong'd by you some
three years since: your worth he says is fam'd, and he doth
nothing doubt but you will do him right, as beseems a souldier.

Bes.

A pox on 'em, so they cry all.

3 Gent.

And a slight note I have about me for you, for the delivery of
which you must excuse me; it is an office that friendship calls
upon me to do, and no way offensive to you; since I desire but
right on both sides.

Bes.

'Tis a challenge Sir, is it not?

3 Gent.

'Tis an inviting to the field.

Bes.

An inviting? O Sir your Mercy, what a Complement he delivers it with? he might as agreeable to my nature present me poison with such a speech: um um um reputation, um um um call you to account, um um um forc'd to this, um um um with my Sword, um um um like a Gentleman, um um um dear to me, um um um satisfaction: 'Tis very well Sir, I do accept it, but he must await an answer this thirteen weeks.

3 Gent.

Why Sir, he would be glad to wipe off his stain as soon as he could.

Bes.

Sir upon my credit I am already ingag'd to two hundred, and twelve, all which must have their stains wip'd off, if that be the word, before him.

3 Gent.

Sir, if you be truly ingag'd but to one, he shall stay a competent time.

Bes.

Upon my faith Sir, to two hundred and twelve, and I have a spent body, too much bruis'd in battel, so that I cannot fight, I must be plain, above three combats a day: All the kindness I can shew him, is to set him resolvedly in my rowle, the two hundred and thirteenth man, which is something, for I tell you, I think there will be more after him, than before him, I think so; pray you commend me to him, and tell him this.

3 Gent.

I will Sir, good morrow to you.

[*Exit 3 Gent*.

Bes.

Good morrow good Sir. Certainly my safest way were to print my self a coward, with a discovery how I came by my credit, and clap it upon every post; I have received above thirty challenges within this two hours, marry all but the first I put off with ingagement, and by good fortune, the first is no madder of fighting than I, so that that's referred, the place where it must be ended, is four days journey off, and our arbitratours are these: He has chosen a Gentleman in travel, and I have a special friend with a quartain ague, like to hold him this five years, for mine: and when his man comes home, we are to expect my friends health: If they would finde me challenges thus thick, as long as I liv'd, I would have no other living; I can make seven shillings a day o'th' paper to the Grocers: yet I learn nothing by all these but a little skill in comparing of stiles. I do finde evidently, that there is some one Scrivener in this Town, that has a great hand in writing of Challenges, for they are all of a cut, and six of 'em in a hand; and they all end, my reputation is dear to me, and I must require satisfaction: Who's there? more paper I hope, no, 'tis my Lord *Bacurius*, I fear all is not well betwixt us.

Enter Bacurius.
Bac.

Now Captain *Bessus*, I come about a frivolous matter, caus'd by as idle a report: you know you were a coward.

Bes.

Very right.

Bac.

And wronged me.

Bes.

True my Lord.

Bac.

But now people will call you valiant, desertlesly I think, yet for their satisfaction, I will have you fight with me.

Bes.

O my good Lord, my deep Engagements.

Bac.

Tell not me of your Engagements, Captain *Bessus*, it is not to be put off with an excuse: for my own part, I am none of the multitude that believe your conversion from Coward.

Bes.

My Lord, I seek not Quarrels, and this belongs not to me, I am not to maintain it.

Bac.

Who then pray?

Bes.

Bessus the Coward wrong'd you.

Bac.

Right.

Bes.

And shall *Bessus* the Valiant, maintain what *Bessus* the Coward did?

Bac.

I pray thee leave these cheating tricks, I swear thou shalt fight with me, or thou shall be beaten extreamly, and kick'd.

Bes.

Since you provoke me thus far, my Lord, I will fight with you, and by my Sword it shall cost me twenty pound, but I will have my Leg well a week sooner purposely.

Bac.

Your Leg? Why, what ailes your Leg? i'le do a cure on you, stand up.

Bes.

My Lord, this is not Noble in you.

Bac.

What dost thou with such a phrase in thy mouth? I will kick thee out of all good words before I leave thee.

Bes.

My Lord, I take this as a punishment for the offence I did when I was a Coward.

Bac.

When thou wert? Confess thy self a Coward still, or by this light, I'le beat thee into Spunge.

Bes.

Why I am one.

Bac.

Are you so Sir? And why do you wear a Sword then?
Come unbuckle.

Bes.

My Lord.

Bac.

Unbuckle I say, and give it me, or as I live, thy head will ake
extreamly.

Bes.

It is a pretty Hilt, and if your Lordship take an affection to
it, with all my heart I present it to you for a New-years-gift.

Bac.

I thank you very heartily, sweet Captain, farewel.

Bes.

One word more, I beseech your Lordship to render me my knife
again.

Bac.

Marry by all means Captain; cherish your self with it, and eat
hard, good Captain; we cannot tell whether we shall have any more
such: Adue dear Captain.

A King, and No King

[*Exit* Bac.

***Bes*.**

I will make better use of this, than of my Sword: A base spirit
has this vantage of a brave one, it keeps always at a stay,
nothing brings it down, not beating. I remember I promis'd the
King in a great Audience, that I would make my back-biters eat my
sword to a knife; how to get another sword I know not, nor know
any means left for me to maintain my credit, but impudence:
therefore I will out-swear him and all his followers, that this
is all that's left uneaten of my sword.

[*Exit* Bessus.

Enter Mardonius.

***Mar*.**

I'le move the King, he is most strangely alter'd; I guess the
cause I fear too right, Heaven has some secret end in't, and 'tis
a scourge no question justly laid upon him: he has followed me
through twenty Rooms; and ever when I stay to wait his command,
he blushes like a Girl, and looks upon me, as if modesty kept in
his business: so turns away from me, but if I go on, he follows
me again.

Enter Arbaces.

See, here he is. I do not use this, yet I know not how, I cannot
chuse but weep to see him; his very Enemies I think, whose wounds

have bred his fame, if they should see him now, would find tears i'their eyes.

Arb.

I cannot utter it, why should I keep
A breast to harbour thoughts? I dare not speak.
Darkness is in my bosom, and there lie
A thousand thoughts that cannot brook the light:
How wilt thou vex 'em when this deed is done,
Conscience, that art afraid to let me name it?

Mar.

How do you Sir?

Arb.

Why very well *Mardonius*, how dost thou do?

Mar.

Better than you I fear.

Arb.

I hope thou art; for to be plain with thee,
Thou art in Hell else, secret scorching flames
That far transcend earthly material fires
Are crept into me, and there is no cure.
Is it not strange *Mardonius*, there's no cure?

Mar.

Sir, either I mistake, or there is something hid
That you would utter to me.

Arb.

So there is, but yet I cannot do it.

Mar.

Out with it Sir, if it be dangerous, I will not shrink to do you
service, I shall not esteem my life a weightier matter than
indeed it is, I know it is subject to more chances than it has
hours, and I were better lose it in my Kings cause, than with an
ague, or a fall, or sleeping, to a Thief; as all these are
probable enough: let me but know what I shall do for you.

Arb.

It will not out: were you with *Gobrias*,
And bad him give my Sister all content
The place affords, and give her leave to send
And speak to whom she please?

Mar.

Yes Sir, I was.

Arb.

And did you to *Bacurius* say as much
About *Tigranes*?

Mar.

Yes.

Arb.

That's all my business.

Mar.

O say not so,
You had an answer of this before;
Besides I think this business might
Be utter'd more carelesly.

Arb.

Come thou shalt have it out, I do beseech thee
By all the love thou hast profest to me,
To see my Sister from me.

Mar.

Well, and what?

Arb.

That's all.

Mar.

That's strange, I shall say nothing to her?

Arb.

Not a word;
But if thou lovest me, find some subtil way
To make her understand by signs.

Mar.

But what shall I make her understand?

Arb.

O *Mardonius*, for that I must be pardon'd.

Mar.

You may, but I can only see her then.

Arb.

'Tis true;
Bear her this Ring then, and
One more advice, thou shall speak to her:
Tell her I do love My kindred all: wilt thou?

Mar.

Is there no more?

Arb.

O yes and her the best;
Better than any Brother loves his Sister: That's all.

Mar.

Methinks this need not have been delivered with such a caution;
I'le do it.

Arb.

There is more yet,
Wilt thou be faith[f]ul to me?

Mar.

Sir, if I take upon me to deliver it, after I hear it, I'le pass
through fire to do it.

Arb.

I love her better than a Brother ought;
Dost thou conceive me?

Mar.

I hope you do not Sir.

Arb.

No, thou art dull, kneel down before her,
And ne'r rise again, till she will love me.

Mar.

Why, I think she does.

Arb.

But better than she does, another way;
As wives love Husbands.

Mar.

Why, I think there are few Wives that love their
Husbands better than she does you.

Arb.

Thou wilt not understand me: is it fit
This should be uttered plainly? take it then
Naked as it is: I would desire her love
Lasciviously, lewdly, incestuously,
To do a sin that needs must damn us both,
And thee too: dost thou understand me now?

Mar.

Yes, there's your Ring again; what have I done
Dishonestly in my whole life, name it,
That you should put so base a business to me?

Arb.

Didst thou not tell me thou wouldst do it?

Mar.

Yes; if I undertook it, but if all

My hairs were lives, I would not be engag'd
In such a case to save my last life.

Arb.

O guilt! ha how poor and weak a thing art thou!
This man that is my servant, whom my breath
Might blow upon the world, might beat me here
Having this cause, whil'st I prest down with sin
Could not resist him: hear ***Mardonius***,
It was a motion mis-beseeming man,
And I am sorry for it.

Mar.

Heaven grant you may be so: you must understand, nothing that you
can utter, can remove my love and service from my Prince. But
otherwise, I think I shall not love you more. For you are sinful,
and if you do this crime, you ought to have no Laws. For after
this, it will be great injustice in you to punish any offender
for any crime. For my self I find my heart too big: I feel I have
not patience to look on whilst you run these forbidden courses.
Means I have none but your favour, and I am rather glad that I
shall lose 'em both together, than keep 'em with such conditions;
I shall find a dwelling amongst some people, where though our
Garments perhaps be courser, we shall be richer far within, and
harbour no such vices in 'em: the Gods preserve you, and mend.

Arb.

Mardonius, stay ***Mardonius***, for though
My present state requires nothing but knaves

To be about me, such as are prepar'd
For every wicked act, yet who does know
But that my loathed Fate may turn about,
And I have use for honest men again?
I hope I may, I prethee leave me not.

Enter Bessus.

Bes.

Where is the King?

Mar.

There.

Bes.

An't please your Majesty, there's the knife.

Arb.

What knife?

Bes.

The Sword is eaten.

Mar.

Away you fool, the King is serious,
And cannot now admit your vanities.

Bes.

Vanities! I'me no honest man, if my enemies have not brought it to this, what, do you think I lie?

Arb.

No, no, 'tis well *Bessus*, 'tis very well I'm glad on't.

Mar.

If your enemies brought it to this, your enemies are Cutlers, come leave the King.

Bes.

Why, may not valour approach him?

Mar.

Yes, but he has affairs, depart, or I shall be something unmannerly with you.

Arb.

No, let him stay *Mardonius*, let him stay,
I have occasion with him very weighty,
And I can spare you now.

Mar.

Sir?

Arb.

Why I can spare you now.

Bes.

Mardonius give way to these State affairs.

Mar.

Indeed you are fitter for this present purpose.

[*Exit* Mar.

Arb.

Bessus, I should imploy thee, wilt thou do't?

Bes.

Do't for you? by this Air I will do any thing without exception, be it a good, bad, or indifferent thing.

Arb.

Do not swear.

Bes.

By this light but I will, any thing whatsoever.

Arb.

But I shall name the thing,
Thy Conscience will not suffer thee to do.

Bes.

I would fain hear that thing.

Arb.

Why I would have thee get my Sister for me?
Thou understandst me, in a wicked manner.

Bes.

O you would have a bout with her?
I'le do't, I'le do't, I'faith.

Arb.

Wilt thou, do'st thou make no more on't? Bes. More? no, why is there any thing else? if there be, it shall be done too.

Arb.

Hast thou no greater sense of such a sin?
Thou art too wicked for my company,
Though I have hell within me, thou may'st yet
Corrupt me further: pray thee answer me,
How do I shew to thee after this motion?

Bes.

Why your Majesty looks as well in my opinion, as ever you did since you were born.

Arb.

But thou appear'st to me after thy grant,
The ugliest, loathed detestable thing
That I ever met with. Thou hast eyes
Like the flames of *Sulphur*, which me thinks do dart
Infection on me, and thou hast a mouth
Enough to take me in where there do stand
Four rows of Iron Teeth.

Bes.

I feel no such thing, but 'tis no matter how I look, Pie do my business as well as they that look better, and when this is dispatch'd, if you have a mind to your Mother, tell me, and you shall see I'le set it hard.

Arb.

My Mother! Heaven forgive me to hear this,
I am inspir'd with horrour: now I hate thee
Worse than my sin, which if I could come by
Should suffer death Eternal ne're to rise
In any breast again. Know I will die
Languishing mad, as I resolve, I shall,
E're I will deal by such an instrument:
Thou art too sinful to imploy in this;
Out of the World, away.

Bes.

What do you mean, Sir?

Arb.

Hung round with Curses, take thy fearful flight
Into the Desarts, where 'mongst all the Monsters
If thou find'st one so beastly as thy self,
Thou shalt be held as innocent.

Bes.

Good Sir.

Arb.

If there were no such instruments as thou,
We Kings could never act such wicked deeds:
Seek out a man that mocks Divinity,
That breaks each precept both of God and man,
And natures too, and does it without lust,
Meerly because it is a law, and good,
And live with him: for him thou canst not spoil.
Away I say, I will not do this sin.

[*Exit* Bessus.

I'le press it here, till it do break my breast,
It heaves to get out, but thou art a sin,
And spight of torture I will keep thee in.

ACTUS QUARTUS.

Enter Gobrias, Panthea, *and* Spaconia.

Gob.

Have you written Madam?

Pan.

Yes, good *Gobrias*.

Gob.

And with a kindness, and such winning words
As may provoke him, at one instant feel
His double fault, your wrong, and his own rashness?

Pan.

I have sent words enough, if words may win him
From his displeasure; and such words I hope,
As shall gain much upon his goodness, *Gobrias*.
Yet fearing they are many, and a womans,
A poor belief may follow, I have woven
As many truths within 'em to speak for me,
That if he be but gracious, and receive 'em--

Gob.

Good Lady be not fearful, though he should not

Give you your present end in this, believe it,
You shall feel, if your vertue can induce you
To labour on't, this tempest which I know,
Is but a poor proof 'gainst your patience:
All those contents, your spirit will arrive at,
Newer and sweeter to you; your Royal brother,
When he shall once collect himself, and see
How far he has been asunder from himself;
What a meer stranger to his golden temper:
Must from those roots of vertue, never dying,
Though somewhat stopt with humour, shoot again
Into a thousand glories, bearing his fair branches
High as our hopes can look at, straight as justice,
Loaden with ripe contents; he loves you dearly,
I know it, and I hope I need not farther
Win you to understand it.

Pan.

I believe it.
But howsoever, I am sure I love him dearly:
So dearly, that if any thing I write
For my enlarging should beget his anger,
Heaven be a witness with me and my faith,
I had rather live intomb'd here.

Gob.

 You shall not feel a worse stroke than your grief,
I am sorry 'tis so sharp, I kiss your hand,
And this night will deliver this true story,
With this hand to your Brother.

Pan.

Peace go with you, you are a good man.

[*Exit* Gob.

My *Spaconia*, why are you ever sad thus?

Spa.

O dear Lady.

Pan.

Prethee discover not a way to sadness,
Nearer than I have in me, our two sorrows
Work like two eager Hawks, who shall get highest;
How shall I lessen thine? for mine I fear
Is easier known than cur'd.

Spa.

Heaven comfort both,
And give you happy ends, however I
Fall in my stubborn fortunes.

Pan.

This but teaches
How to be more familiar with our sorrows,
That are too much our masters: good *Spaconia*
How shall I do you service?

Spa.

Noblest Lady,
You make me more a slave still to your goodness,
And only live to purchase thanks to pay you,
For that is all the business of my life: now
I will be bold, since you will have it so,
To ask a noble favour of you.

Pan.

Speak it, 'tis yours, for from so sweet a vertue,
No ill demand has issue.

Spa.

Then ever vertuous, let me beg your will
In helping me to see the Prince *Tigranes*,
With whom I am equal prisoner, if not more.

Pan.

Reserve me to a greater end *Spaconia*;
Bacurius cannot want so much good manners
As to deny your gentle visitation,
Though you came only with your own command.

Spa.

I know they will deny me gracious Madam,
Being a stranger, and so little fam'd,
So utter empty of those excellencies
That tame Authority; but in you sweet Lady,

All these are natural; beside, a power
Deriv'd immediate from your Royal brother,
Whose least word in you may command the Kingdom.

Pan.

More than my word *Spaconia*, you shall carry,
For fear it fail you.

Spa.

Dare you trust a Token?
Madam I fear I am grown too bold a begger.

Pan.

You are a pretty one, and trust me Lady
It joyes me, I shall do a good to you,
Though to my self I never shall be happy:
Here, take this Ring, and from me as a Token
Deliver it; I think they will not stay you:
So all your own desires go with you Lady.

Spa.

And sweet peace to your Grace.

Pan.

Pray Heaven I find it.

[*Exeunt*.

Enter Tigranes, *in prison*.

Tigr.

Fool that I am, I have undone my self,
And with my own hand turn'd my fortune round,
That was a fair one: I have childishly
Plaid with my hope so long, till I have broke it,
And now too late I mourn for't; O *Spaconia*!
Thou hast found an even way to thy revenge now,
Why didst thou follow me like a faint shadow,
To wither my desires? But wretched fool,
Why did I plant thee 'twixt the Sun and me,
To make me freeze thus? Why did I prefer her
To the fair Princess? O thou fool, thou fool,
Thou family of fools, live like a slave still,
And in thee bear thine own hell and thy torment,
Thou hast deserv'd: Couldst thou find no Lady
But she that has thy hopes to put her to,
And hazard all thy peace? None to abuse,
But she that lov'd thee ever? poor *Spaconia*,
And so much lov'd thee, that in honesty
And honour thou art bound to meet her vertues:
She that forgot the greatness of her grief
And miseries, that must follow such mad passions,
Endless and wild as women; she that for thee
And with thee left her liberty, her name,
And Country, you have paid me equal, Heavens,
And sent my own rod to correct me with;
A woman: for inconstancy I'le suffer,
Lay it on justice, till my soul melt in me
For my unmanly, beastly, sudden doting
Upon a new face: after all my oaths

A King, and No King

Many and strange ones,
I feel my old fire flame again and burn
So strong and violent, that should I see her
Again, the grief and that would kill me.

Enter Bacurius *And* Spaconia.

Bac.

Lady, your token I acknowledge, you may pass;
There is the King.

Spa.

I thank your Lordship for it.

[*Exit* Bac.

Tigr.

She comes, she comes, shame hide me ever from her,
Would I were buried, or so far remov'd
Light might not find me out, I dare not see her.

Spa.

Nay never hide your self; or were you hid
Where earth hides all her riches, near her Center;
My wrongs without more day would light me to you:
I must speak e're I die; were all your greatness
Doubled upon you, y'are a perjur'd man,
And only mighty in your wickedness
Of wronging women. Thou art false, false Prince;

I live to see it, poor *Spaconia* lives
To tell thee thou art false; and then no more;
She lives to tell thee thou art more unconstant,
Than all ill women ever were together.
Thy faith is firm as raging over-flowes,
That no bank can command; as lasting
As boyes gay bubbles, blown i'th' Air and broken:
The wind is fixt to thee: and sooner shall
The beaten Mariner with his shrill whistle
Calm the loud murmur of the troubled main,
And strike it smooth again; than thy soul fall
To have peace in love with any: Thou art all
That all good men must hate; and if thy story
Shall tell succeeding ages what thou wert,
O let it spare me in it, lest true lovers
In pity of my wrong, burn thy black Legend,
And with their curses, shake thy sleeping ashes.

Tigr.

Oh! oh!

Spa.

The destinies, I hope, have pointed out
Our ends, that thou maist die for love,
Though not for me; for this assure thy self,
The Princess hates thee deadly, and will sooner
Be won to marry with a Bull, and safer
Than such a beast as thou art: I have struck,
I fear, too deep; beshrow me for't; Sir,
This sorrow works me like a cunning friendship,
Into the same piece with it; 'tis asham'd,

Alas, I have been too rugged: Dear my Lord,
I am sorry I have spoken any thing,
Indeed I am, that may add more restraint
To that too much you have: good Sir, be pleas'd
To think it was a fault of love, not malice;
And do as I will do, forgive it Prince.
I do, and can forgive the greatest sins
To me you can repent of; pray believe.

Tigr.

O my *Spaconia*! O thou vertuous woman!

Spa.

Nay, more, the King Sir.

Enter Arbaces, Bacurius, Mardonius.

Arb.

Have you been carefull of our noble Prisoner,
That he want nothing fitting for his greatness?

Bac.

I hope his grace will quit me for my care Sir.

Arb.

'Tis well, royal *Tigranes*, health.

***Tigr*.**

More than the strictness of this place can give Sir,
I offer back again to great ***Arbaces***.

***Arb*.**

We thank you worthy Prince, and pray excuse us,
We have not seen you since your being here,
I hope your noble usage has been equall
With your own person: your imprisonment,
If it be any, I dare say is easie,
And shall not last t[w]o dayes.

***Tigr*.**

I thank you;
My usage here has been the same it was,
Worthy a royal Conqueror. For my restraint,
It came unkindly, because much unlook'd for;
But I must bear it.

***Arb*.**

What Lady's that? ***Bacurius***?

***Bac*.**

One of the Princess women, Sir.

***Arb*.**

I fear'd it, why comes she hither?

Bac.

To speak with the Prince *Tigranes*.

Arb.

From whom, *Bacurius*?

Bac.

From the Princess, Sir.

Arb.

I knew I had seen her.

Mar.

His fit begins to take him now again,
'Tis a strange Feaver, and 'twill shake us all anon, I fear,
Would he were well cur'd of this raging folly:

Give me the warrs, where men are mad, and may talk what they list, and held the bravest fellows; This pelting prating peace is good for nothing: drinking's a vertue to't.

Arb.

I see there's truth in no man, nor obedience,
But for his own ends, why did you let her in?

Bac.

It was your own command to barr none from him,
Besides, the Princess sent her ring Sir, for my warrant.

Arb.

A token to *Tigranes*, did she not?
Sir tell truth.

Bac.

I do not use to lie Sir,
'Tis no way I eat or live by, and I think,
This is no token Sir.

Mar.

This combat has undone him: if he had been well beaten, he had been temperate; I shall never see him handsome again, till he have a Horse-mans staffe yok'd thorow his shoulders, or an arm broken with a bullet.

Arb.

I am trifled with.

Bac.

Sir?

Arb.

I know it, as I know thee to be false.

Mar.

Now the clap comes.

Bac.

You never knew me so, Sir I dare speak it,
And durst a worse man tell me, though my better--

Mar.

'Tis well said, by my soul.

Arb.

Sirra, you answer as you had no life.

Bac.

That I fear Sir to lose nobly.

Arb.

I say Sir, once again.

Bac.

You may say what yo[u] please, Sir,
Would I might do so.

Arb.

I will, Sir, and say openly, this woman carries letters,
By my life I know she carries letters, this woman does it.

Mar.

Would **Bessus** were here to take her aside and search her, He would quickly tell you what she carried Sir.

Arb.

I have found it out, this woman carries letters.

Mar.

If this hold, 'twill be an ill world for Bawdes, Chamber-maids and Post-boyes, I thank heaven I have none I but his letters patents, things of his own enditing.

Arb.

Prince, this cunning cannot do't.

Tigr.

Doe, What Sir? I reach you not.

Arb.

It shall not serve your turn, Prince.

Tigr.

Serve my turn Sir?

Arb.

I Sir, it shall not serve your turn.

Tigr.

Be plainer, good Sir.

Arb.

This woman shall carry no more letters back to your
Love ***Panthea***, by Heaven she shall not, I say she shall not.

Mar.

This would make a Saint swear like a souldier.

Tigr.

This beats me more, King, than the blowes you gave me.

Arb.

Take'em away both, and together let them prisoners be, strictly
and closely kept, or Sirra, your life shall answer it, and let
no body speak with'em hereafter.

Tigr.

Well, I am subject to you,
And must indure these passions:
This is the imprisonment I have look'd for always.
And the dearer place I would choose.

[*Exeunt* Tigr. Spa. Bac.

Mar.

Sir, you have done well now.

Arb.

Dare you reprove it?

Mar.

No.

Arb.

You must be crossing me.

Mar.

I have no letters Sir to anger you,
But a dry sonnet of my Corporals
To an old Suttlers wife, and that I'll burn, Sir.
'Tis like to prove a fine age for the Ignorant.

Arb.

How darst thou so often forfeit thy life?
Thou know'st 'tis in my power to take it.

Mar.

Yes, and I know you wo'not, or if you doe, you'll miss it quickly.

Arb.

Why?

Mar.

Who shall tell you of these childish follies
When I am dead? who shall put to his power
To draw those vertues out of a flood of humors,
When they are drown'd, and make'em shine again?
No, cut my head off:
Then you may talk, and be believed, and grow worse,
And have your too self-glorious temper rot
Into a deep sleep, and the Kingdom with you,
Till forraign swords be in your throats, and slaughter
Be every where about you like your flatterers.
Do, kill me.

Arb.

Prethee be tamer, good **Mardonius**,
Thou know'st I love thee, nay I honour thee,
Believe it good old Souldier, I am thine;

But I am rack'd clean from my self, bear with me,
Woot thou bear with me my *Mardonius?*

Enter Gobrias.

Mar.

There comes a good man, love him too, he's temperate,
You may live to have need of such a vertue,
Rage is not still in fashion.

Arb.

Welcome good *Gobrias*.

Gob.

My service and this letter to your Grace.

Arb.

From whom?

Gob.

From the rich Mine of vertue and beauty,
Your mournfull Sister.

Arb.

She is in prison, *Gobrias,* is she not?

Gob.

She is Sir, till your pleasure to enlarge her,
Which on my knees I beg. Oh 'tis not fit,
That all the sweetness of the world in one,
The youth and vertue that would tame wild Tygers,
And wilder people, that have known no manners,
Should live thus cloistred up; for your loves sake,
If there be any in that noble heart,
To her a wretched Lady, and forlorn,
Or for her love to you, which is as much
As nature and obedience ever gave,
Have pity on her beauties.

Arb.

Pray thee stand up; 'Tis true, she is too fair,
And all these commendations but her own,
Would thou had'st never so commended her,
Or I nere liv'd to have heard it *Gobrias;*
If thou but know'st the wrong her beautie does her,
Thou wouldst in pity of her be a lyar,
Thy ignorance has drawn me wretched man,
Whither my self nor thou canst well tell: O my fate!
I think she loves me, but I fear another
Is deeper in her heart: How thinkst thou *Gobrias*?

Gob.

I do beseech your Grace believe it not,
For let me perish if it be not false. Good Sir, read her Letter.

Mar.

This Love, or what a devil it is I know not, begets more mischief than a Wake. I had rather be well beaten, starv'd, or lowsie, than live within the Air on't. He that had seen this brave fellow Charge through a grove of Pikes but t'other day, and look upon him now, will ne'r believe his eyes again: if he continue thus but two days more, a Taylor may beat him with one hand tied behind him.

Arb.

Alas, she would be at liberty.
And there be a thousand reasons *Gobrias,*
Thousands that will deny't:
Which if she knew, she would contentedly
Be where she is: and bless her vertues for it,
And me, though she were closer, she would, *Gobrias,*
Good man indeed she would.

Gob.

Then good Sir, for her satisfaction,
Send for her and with reason make her know
Why she must live thus from you.

Arb.

I will; go bring her to me.

                        [*Exeunt all.*

Enter Bessus, *And two Sword-men, and a Boy.*

Bes.

Y'are very welcome both; some stools boy,
And reach a Table; Gentlemen o'th' Sword,
Pray sit without more complement; be gone child.
I have been curious in the searching of you,
Because I understand you wise and valiant persons.

1.

We understand our selves Sir.

Bes.

Nay Gentlemen, and dear friends o'th' Sword,
No complement I pray, but to the cause
I hang upon, which in few, is my honour.

2.

You cannot hang too much Sir, for your honour,
But to your cause.

Bes.

Be wise, and speak truth, my first doubt is,
My beating by my Prince.

1.

Stay there a little Sir, do you doubt a beating?
Or have you had a beating by your Prince?

***Bes*.**

Gentlemen o'th' Sword, my Prince has beaten me.

2.

Brother, what think you of this case?

1.

If he has beaten him, the case is clear.

2.

If he have beaten him, I grant the case;
But how? we cannot be too subtil in this business,
I say, but how?

***Bes*.**

Even with his Royal hand.

1.

Was it a blow of love, or indignation?

***Bes*.**

'Twas twenty blows of indignation, Gentlemen,
Besides two blows o'th face.

2.

Those blows o'th' face have made a new cause on't,
The rest were but an horrible rudeness.

1.

Two blows o'th' face, and given by a worse man, I must confess,
as the Sword-men say, had turn'd the business: Mark me brother,
by a worse man; but being by his Prince, had they been ten, and
those ten drawn teeth, besides the hazard of his nose for ever;
all this had been but favours: this is my flat opinion, which
I'le die in.

2.

The King may do much Captain, believe it; for had he crackt your
Scull through, like a bottle, or broke a Rib or two with tossing
of you, yet you had lost no honour: This is strange you may
imagine, but this is truth now Captain.

Bes.

I will be glad to embrace it Gentlemen;
But how far may he strike me?

1.

There is another: a new cause rising from the time and distance,
in which I will deliver my opinion: he may strike, beat, or cause
to be beaten: for these are natural to man: your Prince, I say,
may beat you, so far forth as his dominion reacheth, that's for
the distance; the time, ten miles a day, I take it.

2.

Brother, you err, 'tis fifteen miles a day,
His stage is ten, his beatings are fifteen.

Bes.

'Tis the longest, but we subjects must--

1.

Be subject to it; you are wise and vertuous.

Bes.

Obedience ever makes that noble use on't,
To which I dedicate my beaten body;
I must trouble you a little further, Gentlemen o'th' Sword.

2.

No trouble at all to us Sir, if we may
Profit your understanding, we are bound
By vertue of our calling to utter our opinions,
Shortly, and discreetly.

Bes.

My sorest business is, I have been kick'd.

2.

How far Sir?

Bes.

Not to flatter my self in it, all over, my sword forc'd but not
lost; for discreetly I rendred it to save that imputation.

1.

It shew'd discretion, the best part of valour.

2.

Brother, this is a pretty cause, pray ponder on't;
Our friend here has been kick'd.

1.

He has so, brother.

2.

Sorely he saies: Now, had he set down here
Upon the meer kick, 't had been Cowardly.

1.

I think it had been Cowardly indeed.

2.

But our friend has redeem'd it in delivering
His sword without compulsion; and that man
That took it of him, I pronounce a weak one,
And his kicks nullities.

He should have kick'd him after the delivering
Which is the confirmation of a Coward.

1.

Brother, I take it, you mistake the question;
For, say that I were kick'd.

2.

I must not say so;
Nor I must not hear it spoke by the tongue of man.
You kick'd, dear brother! you're merry.

1.

But put the case I were kick'd?

2.

Let them put it that are things weary of their lives, and know not honour; put the case you were kick'd?

1.

I do not say I was kickt.

2.

Nor no silly creature that wears his head without a Case, his soul in a Skin-coat: You kickt dear brother?

Bes.

Nay Gentlemen, let us do what we shall do,
Truly and honest[l]y; good Sirs to the question.

1.

Why then I say, suppose your Boy kick't, Captain?

2.

The Boy may be suppos'd is liable.

1.

A foolish forward zeal Sir, in my friend;
But to the Boy, suppose the Boy were kickt.

Bes.

I do suppose it.

1.

Has your Boy a sword?

Bes.

Surely no; I pray suppose a sword too.

1.

I do suppose it; you grant your Boy was kick't then.

2.

By no means Captain, let it be supposed still; the word grant, makes not for us.

1.

I say this must be granted.

2

This must be granted brother?

1.

I, this must be granted.

2.

Still this must?

1.

I say this must be granted.

2.

I, give me the must again, brother, you palter.

1.

I will not hear you, wasp.

2.

Brother, I say you palter, the must three times together; I wear as sharp Steel as another man, and my Fox bites as deep, musted, my dear brother. But to the cause again.

***Bes*.**

Nay look you Gentlemen.

2.

In a word, I ha' done.

1.

A tall man but intemperate, 'tis great pity;
Once more suppose the Boy kick'd.

2.

Forward.

1.

And being thorowly kick'd, laughs at the kicker.

2

So much for us; proceed.

1.

And in this beaten scorn, as I may call it,
Delivers up his weapon; where lies the error?

Bes.

It lies i'th' beating Sir, I found it four dayes since.

2.

The error, and a sore one as I take it,
Lies in the thing kicking.

Bes.

I understand that well, 'tis so indeed Sir.

1.

That is according to the man that did it.

2.

There springs a new branch, whose was the foot?

Bes.

A Lords.

1.

The cause is mighty, but had it been two Lords,

And both had kick'd you, if you laugh, 'tis clear.

Bes.

I did laugh,
But how will that help me, Gentlemen?

2.

Yes, it shall help you if you laught aloud.

Bes.

As loud as a kick'd man could laugh, I laught Sir.

1.

My reason now, the valiant man is known
By suffering and contemning; you have
Enough of both, and you are valiant.

2.

If he be sure he has been kick'd enough:
For that brave sufferance you speak of brother,
Consists not in a beating and away,
But in a cudgell'd body, from eighteen
To eight and thirty; in a head rebuk'd
With pots of all size, degrees, stools, and bed-staves,
This showes a valiant man.

Bes.

Then I am valiant, as valiant as the proudest,
For these are all familiar things to me;
Familiar as my sleep, or want of money,
All my whole body's but one bruise with beating,
I think I have been cudgell'd with all nations,
And almost all Religions.

2.

Embrace him brother, this man is valiant,
I know it by my self, he's valiant.

1.

Captain, thou art a valiant Gentleman,
To bide upon, a very valiant man.

Bes.

My equall friends o'th'Sword, I must request your hands to this.

2.

'Tis fit it should be.

Bes.

Boy, get me some wine, and pen and Ink within:
Am I clear, Gentlemen?

1.

Sir, the world has taken notice what we have done,
Make much of your body, for I'll pawn my steel,
Men will be coyer of their legs hereafter.

Bes.

I must request you goe along and testife to the Lord *Bacurius*,
whose foot has struck me, how you find my cause.

2.

We will, and tell that Lord he must be rul'd,
Or there are those abroad, will rule his Lordship.

[*Exeunt.*

Enter Arbaces **at one door, and** Gob. **and** Panthea at another.

Gob.

Sir, here's the Princess.

Arb.

Leave us then alone,
For the main cause of her imprisonment
Must not be heard by any but her self.

[*Exit* Gob.

You're welcome Sister, and would to heaven
I could so bid you by another name:
If you above love not such sins as these,
Circle my heart with thoughts as cold as snow
To quench these rising flames that harbour here.

[P]an.

Sir, does it please you I should speak?

Arb.

Please me?
I, more than all the art of musick can,
Thy speech doth please me, for it ever sounds,
As thou brought'st joyfull unexpected news;
And yet it is not fit thou shouldst be heard.
I pray thee think so.

Pan.

Be it so, I will.
Am I the first that ever had a wrong
So far from being fit to have redress,
That 'twas unfit to hear it? I will back
To prison, rather than disquiet you,
And wait till it be fit.

Arb.

No, do not goe;
For I will hear thee with a serious thought:
I have collected all that's man about me

Together strongly, and I am resolv'd
To hear thee largely, but I do beseech thee,
Do not come nearer to me, for there is
Something in that, that will undoe us both.

Pan.

Alas Sir, am I venome?

Arb.

Yes, to me;
Though of thy self I think thee to be
In equall degree of heat or cold,
As nature can make: yet as unsound men
Convert the sweetest and the nourishing'st meats
Into diseases; so shall I distemper'd,
Do thee, I pray thee draw no nearer to me.

Pan.

Sir, this is that I would: I am of late
Shut from the world, and why it should be thus,
Is all I wish to know.

Arb.

Why credit me *Panthea*,
Credit me that am thy brother,
Thy loving brother, that there is a cause
Sufficient, yet unfit for thee to know,
That might undoe thee everlastingly,
Only to hear, wilt thou but credit this?

By Heaven 'tis true, believe it if thou canst.

Pan .

Children and fools are ever credulous,
And I am both, I think, for I believe;
If you dissemble, be it on your head;
I'le back unto my prison: yet me-thinks
I might be kept in some place where you are;
For in my self, I find I know not what
To call it, but it is a great desire
To see you often.

Arb .

Fie, you come in a step, what do you mean?
Dear sister, do not so: Alas ***Panthea***,
Where I am would you be? Why that's the cause
You are imprison'd, that you may not be
Where I am.

Pan .

Then I must indure it Sir, Heaven keep you.

Arb .

Nay, you shall hear the case in short ***Panthea***,
And when thou hear'st it, thou wilt blush for me,
And hang thy head down like a Violet
Full of the mornings dew: There is a way
To gain thy freedome, but 'tis such a one
As puts thee in worse bondage, and I know,

Thou wouldst encounter fire, and make a proof
Whether the gods have care of innocence,
Rather than follow it: Know that I have lost,
The only difference betwixt man and beast,
My reason.

Pan.

Heaven forbid.

Arb.

Nay 'tis gone;
And I am left as far without a bound,
As the wild Ocean, that obeys the winds;
Each sodain passion throwes me where it lists,
And overwhelms all that oppose my will:
I have beheld thee with a lustfull eye;
My heart is set on wickedness to act
Such sins with thee, as I have been afraid
To think of, if thou dar'st consent to this,
Which I beseech thee do not, thou maist gain
Thy liberty, and yield me a content;
If not, thy dwelling must be dark and close,
Where I may never see thee; For heaven knows
That laid this punishment upon my pride,
Thy sight at some time will enforce my madness
To make a start e'ne to thy ravishing;
Now spit upon me, and call all reproaches
Thou canst devise together, and at once
Hurle'em against me: for I am a sickness
As killing as the plague, ready to seize thee.

Pan.

Far be it from me to revile the King:
But it is true, that I shall rather choose
To search out death, that else would search out me,
And in a grave sleep with my innocence,
Than welcome such a sin: It is my fate,
To these cross accidents I was ordain'd,
And must have patience; and but that my eyes
Have more of woman in 'em than my heart,
I would not weep: Peace enter you again.

Arb.

Farwell, and good *Panthea* pray for me,
Thy prayers are pure, that I may find a death
However soon before my passions grow
That they forget what I desire is sin;
For thither they are tending: if that happen,
Then I shall force thee tho' thou wert a Virgin
By vow to Heaven, and shall pull a heap
Of strange yet uninvented sin upon me.

Pan.

Sir, I will pray for you, yet you shall know
It is a sullen fate that governs us,
For I could wish as heartily as you
I were no sister to you, I should then
Imbrace your lawfull love, sooner than health.

Arb.

Couldst thou affect me then?

Pan.

So perfectly,
That as it is, I ne're shall sway my heart,
To like another.

Arb.

Then I curse my birth,
Must this be added to my miseries
That thou art willing too? is there no stop
To our full happiness, but these meer sounds
Brother and Sister?

Pan.

There is nothing else,
But these alas will separate us more
Than twenty worlds betwixt us.

Arb.

I have liv'd
To conquer men and now am overthrown
Only by words Brother and Sister: where
Have those words dwelling? I will find 'em out,
And utterly destroy 'em; but they are
Not to be grasp'd: let 'em be men or beasts,
And I will cut 'em from the Earth, or Towns,

And I will raze 'em, and the[n] blow 'em up:
Let 'em be Seas, and I will drink 'em off,
And yet have unquencht fire left in my breast:
Let 'em be any thing but meerly voice.

Pan.

But 'tis not in the power of any force,
Or policy to conquer them.

Arb.

Panthea, What shall we do?
Shall we stand firmly here, and gaze our eyes out?

Pan.

Would I could do so,
But I shall weep out mine.

Arb.

Accursed man,
Thou bought'st thy reason at too dear a rate,
For thou hast all thy actions bounded in
With curious rules, when every beast is free:
What is there that acknowledges a kindred
But wretched man? Who ever saw the Bull
Fearfully leave the Heifer that he lik'd
Because they had one Dam?

Pan.

Sir, I disturb you and my self too;
'Twere better I were gone.

Arb.

I will not be so foolish as I was,
Stay, we will love just as becomes our births,
No otherwise: Brothers and Sisters may
Walk hand in hand together; so will we,
Come nearer: is there any hurt in this?

Pan.

I hope not.

Arb.

Faith there is none at all:
And tell me truly now, is there not one
You love above me?

Pan.

No by Heaven.

Arb.

Why yet you sent unto *Tigranes*, Sister.

Pan.

True, but for another: for the truth--

Arb.

No more,
I'le credit thee, thou canst not lie,
Thou art all truth.

Pan.

But is there nothing else,
That we may do, but only walk? methinks
Brothers and Sisters lawfully may kiss.

Arb.

And so they may ***Panthea***, so will we,
And kiss again too; we were too scrupulous,
And foolish, but we will be so no more.

Pan.

If you have any mercy, let me go
To prison, to my death, to any thing:
I feel a sin growing upon my blood,
Worse than all these, hotter than yours.

Arb.

That is impossible, what shou'd we do?

Pan.

Flie Sir, for Heavens sake.

Arb.

So we must away,
Sin grows upon us more by this delay.

[***Exeunt several wayes***.

Actus Quintus.

Enter Mardonius **And** Lygones.

Mar.

Sir, the King has seen your Commission, and believes it, and freely by this warrant gives you power to visit Prince Tigranes, your Noble Master.

Lygr.

I thank his Grace and kiss his hand.

Mar.

But is the main of all your business ended in this?

Lyg.

I have another, but a worse, I am asham'd, it is a business.

Mar.

You serve a worthy person, and a stranger I am sure you are; you may imploy me if you please without your purse, such Offices should ever be their own rewards.

Lyg.

I am bound to your Nobleness.

Mar.

I may have need of you, and then this courtesie,
If it be any, is not ill bestowed;
But may I civilly desire the rest?
I shall not be a hurter if no helper.

Lyg.

Sir you shall know I have lost a foolish Daughter,
And with her all my patience, pilfer'd away
By a mean Captain of your Kings.

Mar.

Stay there Sir:
If he have reacht the Noble worth of Captain,
He may well claim a worthy Gentlewoman,
Though she were yours, and Noble.

Lyg.

I grant all that too: but this wretched fellow
Reaches no further than the empty name
That serves to feed him; were he valiant,
Or had but in him any noble nature
That might hereafter promise him a good man,
My cares were so much lighter, and my grave
A span yet from me.

Mar.

I confess such fellows
Be in all Royal Camps, and have and must be,
To make the sin of Coward more detested
In the mean souldier that with such a foil
Sets off much valour. By description
I should now guess him to you, it was ***Bessus***,
I dare almost with confidence pronounce it.

Lyg.

'Tis such a scurvie name as ***Bessus***, and now I think 'tis he.

Mar.

Captain do you call him?
Believe me Sir, you have a misery
Too mighty for your age: A pox upon him,
For that must be the end of all his service:
Your Daughter was not mad Sir?

Lyg.

No, would she had been,
The fault had had more credit: I would do something.

Mar.

I would fain counsel you, but to what I know not, he's so below a beating, that the Women find him not worthy of their Distaves, and to hang him were to cast away a Rope; he's such an Airie, thin unbodyed Coward, that no revenge can catch him: I'le tell you Sir, and tell you truth; this Rascal fears neither God nor man, he has been so beaten: sufferance has made him Wainscot: he has had since he was first a slave, at least three hundred Daggers set in's head, as little boys do new Knives in hot meat, there's not a Rib in's body o' my Conscience that has not been thrice broken with dry beating: and now his sides look like two Wicker Targets, every way bended; Children will shortly take him for a Wall, and set their Stone-bows in his forehead, he is of so base a sense, I cannot in a week imagine what shall be done to him.

Lyg.

Sure I have committed some great sin

That this fellow should be made my Rod,
I would see him, but I shall have no patience.

Mar.

'Tis no great matter if you have not: if a Laming of him, or such a toy may do you pleasure Sir, he has it for you, and I'le help you to him: 'tis no news to him to have a Leg broken, or Shoulder out, with being turn'd o'th' stones like a Tansie: draw not your Sword if you love it; for on my Conscience his head will break it: we use him i'th' Wars like a Ram to shake a wall withal. Here comes the very person of him, do as you shall find your temper, I must leave you: but if you do not break him like a Bisket, you are much to blame Sir.

[*Exit* Mar.

Enter Bessus *And the Sword men*.

Lyg.

Is your name *Bessus*?

Bes.

Men call me Captain Bessus.

Lyg.

Then Ca[p]tain *Bessus*, you are a rank rascall, without more exordiums, a durty frozen slave; and with the favor of your friends here I will beat you.

2 Sword.

Pray use your pleasure Sir,
You seem to be a Gentleman.

Lyg.

Thus Captain **Bessus**, thus; thus twing your nose, thus kick, thus tread you.

Bes.

I do beseech you yield your cause Sir quickly.

Lyg.

Indeed I should have told that first.

Bes.

I take it so.

1 Sword.

Captain, he should indeed, he is mistaken.

Lyg.

Sir, you shall have it quickly, and more beating,
you have stoln away a Lady, Captain coward, and such an one.

beats him.

Bes.

Hold, I beseech you, hold Sir, I never yet stole any living thing that had a tooth about it.

Lyg.

I know you dare lie.

Bes.

With none but Summer Whores upon my life Sir, my means and manners never could attempt above a hedge or hay-cock.

Lyg.

Sirra, that quits not me, where is this Lady? do that you do not use to do; tell truth, or by my hand, I'le beat your Captains brains out, wash'em, and put 'em in again, that will I.

Bes.

There was a Lady Sir, I must confess, once in my charge: the Prince Tigranes gave her to my guard for her safety, how I us'd her, she may her self report, she's with the Prince now: I did but wait upon her like a groom, which she will testife I am sure: if not, my brains are at your service when you please Sir, and glad I have 'em for you.

Lyg.

This is most likely, Sir, I ask you pardon, and am sorry I was so intemperate.

Bes.

Well I can ask no more, you will think it strange not to have me beat you at first sight.

Lyg.

Indeed I would, but I know your goodness can forget twenty beatings, you must forgive me.

Bes.

Yes there's my hand, go where you will, I shall think you a valiant fellow for all this.

Lyg.

My da[u]ghter is a Whore, I feel it now too sensible; yet I will see her, discharge my self from being father to her, and then back to my Country, and there die, farwell Captain.

[*Exit Lygo*.

Bes.

Farwell Sir, farwell, commend me to the gentlewoman I pray.

1 Sword.

How now Captain? bear up man.

Bes.

Gentlemen o'th'sword, your hands once more; I have been kickt agen, but the foolish fellow is penitent, has askt me Mercy, and my honour's safe.

2 Sword.

We knew that, or the foolish fellow had better have kickt his grandsir.

Bes.

Confirm, confirm I pray.

1 Sword.

There be our hands agen, now let him come and say he was not sorry, and he sleeps for it.

Bes.

Alas good ignorant old man, let him go, let him go, these courses will undo him.

[*Exeunt clear.*

Enter Lygones *And* Bacurius.

Bac.

My Lord, your authority is good, and I am glad it is so, for my consent would never hinder you from seeing your own King, I am a

Minister, but not a governor of this State, yonder is your King, I'le leave you.

[*Exit*.

Enter Tigranes *And* Spaconia.

Lyg.

There he is indeed, and with him my disloyal child.

Tigr.

I do perceive my fault so much, that yet me thinks thou shouldst not have forgiven me.

Lyg.

Health to your Majesty.

Tigr.

What? good *Lygones* welcome, what business brought thee hither?

Lyg.

Several businesses. My publick businesses will appear by this, I have a message to deliver, which if it please you so to authorize, is an embassage from the Armenian State, unto Arbaces for your liberty: the offer's there set down, please you to read it.

Tigr.

There is no alteration happened since I came thence?

Lyg.

None Sir, all is as it was.

Tigr.

And all our friends are well?

Lyg.

All very well.

Spa.

Though I have done nothing but what was good, I dare not see my Father, it was fault enough not to acquaint him with that good.

Lyg.

Madam I should have seen you.

Spa.

O good Sir forgive me.

Lyg.

Forgive you, why? I am no kin to you, am I?

Spa.

Should it be measur'd by my mean deserts, indeed you are not.

Lyg.

Thou couldest prate unhappily ere thou couldst go, would thou couldst do as well, and how does your custome hold out here?

Spa.

Sir?

Lyg.

Are you in private still, or how?

Spa.

What do you mean?

Lyg.

Do you take mony? are you come to sell sin yet? perhaps I can help you to liberal Clients: or has not the King cast you off yet? O thou vile creature, whose best commendation is, that thou art a young whore, I would thy Mother had liv'd to see this, or rather that I had died ere I had seen it; why didst not make me acquainted when thou wert first resolv'd to be a whore, I would have seen thy hot lust satisfied more privately: I would have kept a dancer and a whole consort of musicians in my own house only to fiddle thee.

Spa.

Sir, I was never whore.

Lyg.

If thou couldst not say so much for thy self, thou shouldst be carted.

Tigr.

Lygones, I have read it, and I like it, you shall deliver it.

Lyg.

Well Sir, I will: but I have private business with you.

Tigr.

Speak, what is't?

Lyg. How has my age deserv'd so ill of you, that you can pick no strumpets i'th' land, but out of my breed?

Tigr.

Strumpets, good *Lygones*?

Lyg.

Yes, and I wish to have you know, I scorn to get a whore for any prince alive, and yet scorn will not help methinks: my Daughter might have been spar'd, there were enow besides.

Tigr.

May I not prosper but she's innocent as morning light for me, and I dare swear for all the world.

Lyg.

Why is she with you then? can she wait on you better than your man, has she a gift in plucking off your stockings, can she make Cawdles well or cut your cornes? Why do you keep her with you? For a Queen I know you do contemn her, so should I, and every subject else think much at it.

Tigr.

Let 'em think much, but 'tis more firm than earth: thou see'st thy Queen there.

Lyg.

Then have I made a fair hand, I call'd her Whore. If I shall speak now as her Father, I cannot chuse but greatly rejoyce that she shall be a Queen: but if I shall speak to you as a States-man, she were more fit to be your whore.

Tigr.

Get you about your business to **Arbaces**, now you talk idlely.

Lyg.

Yes Sir, I will go, and shall she be a Queen? she had more wit than her old Father, when she ran away: shall she be Queen? now by my troth 'tis fine, I'le dance out of all measure at her wedding: shall I not Sir?

Tigr.

Yes marry shalt thou.

Lyg.

I'le make these withered kexes bear my body two hours together above ground.

Tigr.

Nay go, my business requires hast.

Lyg.

Good Heaven preserve you, you are an excellent King.

Spa.

Farwell good Father.

Lyg.

Farwell sweet vertuous Daughter, I never was so joyfull in all my life, that I remember: shall she be a Queen? Now I perceive a man may weep for joy, I had thought they had lyed that said so.

[*Exit* Lygones.

Tigr.

Come my dear love.

Spa.

But you may see another may alter that again.

Tigr.

Urge it no more, I have made up a new strong constancy, not to be shook with eyes: I know I have the passions of a man, but if I meet with any subject that should hold my eyes more firmly than is fit, I'le think of thee, and run away from it: let that suffice.

[*Exeunt all.*

Enter Bacurius *And his Servant.*

Bac.

Three Gentlemen without to speak with me?

Ser.

Yes Sir.

Bac.

Let them come in.

Enter Bessus *with the two Sword-men.*

Ser.

They are entred Sir already.

Bac.

Now fellows your business? are these the Gentlemen?

Bes.

My Lord, I have made bold to bring these Gentlemen, my friends o'th' Sword along with me.

Bac.

I am afraid you'l fight then.

Bes.

My good Lord, I will not, your Lordship is much mistaken, fear not Lord.

Bac.

Sir, I am sorry for't.

Bes.

I ask no more in honour, Gentlemen you hear my Lord is sorry.

Bac.

Not that I have beaten you, but beaten one that will be beaten:

one whose dull body will require a laming, as Surfeits do the diet, spring and fall; now to your Sword-men; what come they for, good Captain Stock-fish?

Bes.

It seems your Lordship has forgot my name.

Bac.

No, nor your nature neither, though they are things fitter I must confess for any thing, than my remembrance, or any honest mans: what shall these Billets do; be pil'd up in my wood-yard?

Bes.

Your Lordship holds your mirth still, Heaven continue it: but for these Gentlemen, they come--

Bac.

To swear you are a Coward, spare your book, I do believe it.

Bes.

Your Lordship still draws wide, they come to vouch under their valiant hands I am no Coward.

Bac.

That would be a show indeed worth seeing: sirra be wise, and take Mony for this motion, travel with it, and where the name of *Bessus* has been known or a good Coward stirring, 'twill yield

more than a tilting. This will prove more beneficial to you, if
you be thrifty, than your Captainship, and more natural: men of
most valiant hands is this true?

2 Sword.

It is so, most renowned.

Bac.

'Tis somewhat strange.

1 Sword.

Lord, it is strange, yet true; we have examined from your
Lordships foot there, to this mans head, the nature of the
beatings; and we do find his honour is come off clean and
sufficient: this as our swords shall help us.

Bac.

You are much bound to your Bil-bow-men, I am glad you are
straight again Captain; 'twere good you would think on some way
to gratifie them, they have undergone a labour for you, ***Bessus***
would have puzl'd ***hercules*** with all his valour.

2 Sword.

Your Lordship must understand we are no men o'th' Law, that take
pay for our opinions: it is sufficient we have clear'd our
friend.

Bac.

Yet there is something due, which I as toucht in Conscience will discharge Captain; I'le pay this Rent for you.

Bes.

Spare your self my good Lord; my brave friends aim at nothing but the vertue.

Bac.

That's but a cold discharge Sir for the pains.

2 Sword.

O Lord, my good Lord.

Bac.

Be not so modest, I will give you something.

Bes.

They shall dine with your Lordship, that's sufficient.

Bac.

Something in hand the while, you Rogues, you Apple-squires: do you come hither with your botled valour, your windy froth, to limit out my beatings?

1 Sword.

I do beseech your Lordship.

2 Sword.

O good Lord.

Bac.

S'foot-what a heavy of beaten slaves are here! get me a Cudgel sirra, and a tough one.

2 Sword.

More of your foot, I do beseech your Lordship.

Bac.

You shall, you shall dog, and your fellow-beagle.

1 Sword.

O' this side good my Lord.

Bac.

Off with your swords, for if you hurt my foot, I'le have you flead you Rascals.

1 Sword.

Mine's off my Lord.

2 Sword.

I beseech your Lordship stay a little, my strap's tied to my Cod piece-point: now when you please.

Bac.

Captain these are your valiant friends, you long for a little too?

Bes.

I am very well, I humbly thank your Lordship.

Bac.

What's that in your pocket, hurts my Toe you Mungril? Thy Buttocks cannot be so hard, out with it quickly.

2 Sword.

Here 'tis Sir, a small piece of Artillery, that a Gentleman a dear friend of your Lordships sent me with, to get it mended Sir, for if you mark, the nose is somewhat loose.

Bac.

A friend of mine you Rascal? I was never wearier of doing any thing, than kicking these two Foot-balls.

Enter Servant.

***Serv*.**

Here is a good Cudgel Sir.

***Bac*.**

It comes too late I'me weary, pray thee do thou beat them.

***2 Sword*.**

My Lord, this is foul play i'faith, to put a fresh man upon us, men are but men Sir.

***Bac*.**

That jest shall save your bones; Captain, Rally up your rotten Regiment and be gone: I had rather thrash than be bound to kick these Rascals, till they cry'd ho; ***Bessus*** you may put your hand to them now, and then you are quit. Farewel, as you like this, pray visit me again, 'twill keep me in good health.

[***Exit*** Bac.

***2 Sword*.**

H'as a devilish hard foot, I never felt the like.

***1 Sword*.**

Nor I, and yet I am sure I have felt a hundred.

2 Sword.

If he kick thus i'th' Dog-daies, he will be dry foundred: what cure now Captain besides Oyl of Baies?

Bes.

Why well enough I warrant you, you can go.

2 Sword.

Yes, heaven be thanked; but I feel a shrowd ach, sure h'as sprang my huckle-bone.

1 Sword.

I ha' lost a hanch.

Bes.

A little butter, friend a little butter, butter and parseley and a soveraign matter: ***probatum est***.

2 Sword.

Captain we must request your hand now to our honours.

Bes.

Yes marry shall ye, and then let all the world come, we are valiant to our selves, and there's an end.

1 Sword.

Nay then we must be valiant; O my ribs.

2 Sword.

O my small guts, a plague upon these sharp-toed shooes, they are murtherers.

[*Exeunt clear*.

Enter Arbaces *with his sword drawn*.

Arb.

It is resolv'd, I bare it whilst I could, I can no more, I must begin with murther of my friends, and so go on to that incestuous ravishing, and end my life and sins with a forbidden blow, upon my self.

Enter Mardonius.

Mar.

What Tragedy is near? That hand was never wont to draw a sword, but it cry'd dead to something.

Arb.

Mardonius, have you bid *Gobrias* come?

Mar.

How do you Sir?

Arb.

Well, is he coming?

Mar.

Why Sir, are you thus? why do your hands proclaim a lawless War against your self?

Arb.

Thou answerest me one question with an other, is **Gobrias** coming?

Mar.

Sir he is.

Arb.

'Tis well, I can forbear your questions then, be gone.

Mar.

Sir, I have mark't.

Arb.

Mark less, it troubles you and me.

Mar.

You are more variable than you were.

Arb.

It may be so.

Mar.

To day no Hermit could be humbler than you were to us all.

Arb.

And what of this?

Mar.

And now you take new rage into your eyes, as you would look us all out of the Land.

Arb.

I do confess it, will that satisfie? I prethee get thee gone.

Mar.

Sir, I will speak.

Arb.

Will ye?

Mar.

It is my duty. I fear you will kill your self: I am a subject,
and you shall do me wrong in't: 'tis my cause, and I may speak.

Arb.

Thou art not train'd in sin, it seems *Mardonius*: kill my self!
by Heaven I will not do it yet; and when I will, I'le tell thee
then: I shall be such a creature, that thou wilt give me leave
without a word. There is a method in mans wickedness, it grows up
by degrees: I am not come so high as killing of my self, there
are a hundred thousand sins 'twixt me and it, which I must doe,
and I shall come to't at last; but take my oath not now, be
satisfied, and get thee hence.

Mar.

I am sorry 'tis so ill.

Arb.

Be sorry then, true sorrow is alone, grieve by thy
self.

Mar.

I pray you let me see your Sword put up before I go: I'le leave
you then.

Arb.

Why so? what folly is this in thee, is it not as apt to mischief

as it was before? can I not reach it thinkst thou? these are
toyes for Children to be pleas'd with, and not men, now I am safe
you think: I would the book of fate were here, my Sword is not so
sure but I would get it out and mangle that, that all the
destinies should quite forget their fixt decrees, and hast to
make us new, for other fortunes, mine could not be worse, wilt
thou now leave me?

Mar.

Heaven put into your bosome temperate thoughts, I'le leave you
though I fear.

Arb.

Go, thou art honest, why should the hasty error of my youth be so
unpardonable to draw a sin helpless upon me?

Enter Gobrias.

Gob.

There is the King, now it is ripe.

Arb.

Draw near thou guilty man, that art the authour of the loathedst
crime five ages have brought forth, and hear me speak; curses
more incurable, and all the evils mans body or his Spirit can
receive be with thee.

Gob.

Why Sir do you curse me thus?

Arb.

Why do I curse thee? if there be a man subtil in curses, that exceeds the rest, his worst wish on thee, thou hast broke my heart.

Gob.

How Sir, have I preserv'd you from a child, from all the arrows, malice, or ambition could shoot at you, and have I this for my pay?

Arb.

'Tis true, thou didst preserve me, and in that wert crueller than hardned murtherers of infants and their Mothers! thou didst save me only till thou hadst studied out a way how to destroy me cunningly thy self: this was a curious way of torturing.

Gob.

What do you mean?

Arb.

Thou knowst the evils thou hast done to me; dost thou remember all those witching letters thou sent'st unto me to Armenia, fill'd with the praise of my beloved Sister, where thou extol'st her beauty, what had I to do with that? what could her beauty be to me? and thou didst write how well she lov'd me, dost thou remember this? so that I doted something before I saw her.

Gob.

This is true.

Arb.

Is it? and when I was return'd thou knowst thou didst pursue it, till thou woundst me into such a strange and unbeliev'd affection, as good men cannot think on.

Gob.

This I grant, I think I was the cause.

Arb.

Wert thou? Nay more, I think thou meant'st it.

Gob.

Sir, I hate to lie, as I love Heaven and honesty, I did, it was my meaning.

Arb.

Be thine own sad judge, a further condemnation will not need, prepare thy self to dy.

Gob.

Why Sir to dy?

Arb.

Why shouldst thou live? was ever yet offender so impudent, that had a thought of Mercy after confession of a crime like this? get out I cannot where thou hurl'st me in, but I can take revenge, that's all the sweetness left for me.

Gob.

Now is the time, hear me but speak.

Arb.

No, yet I will be far more mercifull than thou wert to me; thou didst steal into me and never gav'st me warning: so much time as I give thee now, had prevented thee for ever. Notwithstanding all thy sins, if thou hast hope, that there is yet a prayer to save thee, turn and speak it to thy self.

Gob.

Sir, you shall know your sins before you do'em, if you kill me.

Arb.

I will not stay then.

Gob.

Know you kill your Father.

Arb.

How?

Gob.

You kill your Father.

Arb.

My Father? though I know't for a lie, made out of fear to save thy stained life; the very reverence of the word comes cross me, and ties mine arm down.

Gob.

I will tell you that shall heighten you again, I am thy Father, I charge thee hear me.

Arb.

If it should be so, as 'tis most false, and that I should be found a Bastard issue, the despised fruit of lawless lust, I should no more admire all my wild passions: but another truth shall be wrung from thee: if I could come by the Spirit of pain, it should be poured on thee, till thou allow'st thy self more full of lies than he that teaches thee.

Enter Arane.

Ara.

Turn thee about, I come to speak to thee thou wicked man, hear me thou tyrant.

Arb.

I will turn to thee, hear me thou Strumpet; I have blotted out the name of Mother, as thou hast thy shame.

Ara.

My shame! thou hast less shame than any thing; why dost thou keep my Daughter in a prison? why dost thou call her Sister, and do this?

Arb.

Cease thy strange impudence, and answer quickly if thou contemnest me, this will ask an answer, and have it.

Ara.

Help me Gentle **Gobrias**.

Arb.

Guilt [dare] not help guilt though they grow together in doing ill, yet at the [punishment] they sever, and each flies the noise of other, think not of help, answer.

Ara.

I will, to what?

Arb.

To such a thing, as if it be a truth think what a creature thou hast made thy self, that didst not shame to do, what I must blush only to ask thee: tell me who I am, whose son I am without all circumstance, be thou as hasty as my Sword will be if thou refusest.

Ara.

Why, you are his son.

Arb.

His Son? swear, swear, thou worse than woman damn'd.

Ara.

By all that's good you are.

Arb.

Then art thou all that ever was known bad, now is the cause of all my strange mis-fortunes come to light: what reverence expectest thou from a child, to bring forth which thou hast offended heaven, thy husband, and the Land? adulterous witch, I know now why thou wouldst have poyson'd me, I was thy lust which thou wouldst have forgot: then wicked Mother of my sins, and me, show me the way to the inheritance I have by thee: which is a spacious world of impious acts, that I may soon possess it: plagues rot thee, as thou liv'st, and such diseases, as use to pay lust, recompence thy deed.

Gob.

You do not know why you curse thus.

Arb.

Too well; you are a pair of Vipers; and behold the Serpent you have got; there is no beast but if he knew it, has a pedigree as brave as mine, for they have more descents, and I am every way as beastly got, as far without the compass of Law as they.

Ara.

You spend your rage and words in vain, and rail upon a guess; hear us a little.

Arb.

No, I will never hear, but talk away my breath, and die.

Gob.

Why, but you are no Bastard.

Arb.

How's that?

Ara.

Nor child of mine.

Arb.

Still you go on in wonders to me.

Gob.

Pray you be more patient, I may bring comfort to you.

Arb.

I will kneel, and hear with the obedience of a child; good Father speak, I do acknowledge you, so you bring comfort.

Gob.

First know, our last King, your supposed Father was old and feeble when he married her, and almost all the Land thought she was past hope of issue from him.

Arb.

Therefore she took leave to play the whore, because the King was old: is this the comfort?

Ara.

What will you find out to give me satisfaction, when you find how you have injur'd me? let fire consume me, if ever I were a whore.

Gob.

For-bear these starts, or I will leave you wedded to despair, as you are now: if you can find a temper, my breath shall be a pleasant western wind that cools and blasts not.

Arb.

Bring it out good Father. I'le lie, and listen here as reverently as to an Angel: if I breath too loud, tell me; for I would be as still as night.

Gob.

Our King I say, was old, and this our Queen desir'd to bring an heir, but yet her husband she thought was past it, and to be dishonest I think she would not: if she would have been, the truth is, she was watcht so narrowly, and had so slender opportunities, she hardly could have been: but yet her cunning found out this way; she feign'd her self with child, and posts were sent in hast throughout the Land, and humble thanks was given in every Church, and prayers were made for her safe going and delivery: she feign'd now to grow bigger, and perceiv'd this hope of issue made her fear'd, and brought a far more large respect from every man, and saw her power increase, and was resolv'd, since she believ'd, she could not hav't indeed, at least she would be thought to have a child.

Arb.

Do I not hear it well? nay I will make no noise at all; but pray you to the point, quickly as you can.

Gob.

Now when the time was full, she should be brought to bed, I had a
Son born, which was you, this the Queen hearing of mov'd me to
let her have you; and such reasons she shewed me, as she knew
would tie my secrecie, she swore you should be King, and to be
short, I did deliver you unto her, and pretended you were dead,
and in mine own house kept a funeral, and had an empty coffin put
in Earth, that night this Queen feign'd hastily to labour and by
a pair of women of her own, which she had charm'd, she made the
world believe she was delivered of you. You grew up as the Kings
Son, till you were six years old; then did the King dye, and did
leave to me Protection of the Realm; and contrary to his own
expectation, left this Queen truely with child indeed, of the
fair Princess ***Panthea***: then she could have torn her hair and
did alone to me, yet durst not speak in publick, for she knew she
should be found a traytor: and her tale would have been thought
madness, or any thing rather than truth. This was the only cause
why she did seek to poyson you, and I to keep you safe; and this
the reason, why I sought to kindle some sparks of love in you to
fair ***Panthea***, that she might get part of her right again.

Arb.

And have you made an end now? is this all? if not,
I will be still till I be aged, till all my hairs be Silver.

Gob.

This is all.

Arb.

And is it true say you too Madam?

Ara.

Yes heaven knows it is most true.

Arb.

Panthea then is not my Sister?

Gob.

No.

Arb. But can you prove this?

Gob.

If you will give consent, else who dares go about it?

Arb.

Give consent? why I will have 'em all that know it rackt, to get this from 'em, all that wait without, come in, what ere you be, come in and be partakers of my joy, O you are welcome.

Enter Bessus, Gentlemen, Mardonius, **And other attendants**.

Arb.

The best news, nay draw no nearer, they all shall hear it, I am found no King.

Mar.

Is that so good news?

Arb.

Yes the happiest news that ere was heard.

Mar.

Indeed 'twere well for you if you might be a little less obey'd.

Arb.

One call the Queen.

Mar.

Why she is there.

Arb.

The Queen *Mardonius*, *Panthea* is the Queen and I am plain *Arbaces*; go some one, she is in *Gobrias* house, since I saw you there are a thousand things delivered to me, you little dream of.

[*Exit a Gent.*

Mar.

So it should seem my Lord, what fury's this?

Gob.

Believe me 'tis no fury, all that he saies is truth.

Mar.

'Tis very strange.

Arb.

Why do you keep your hats off Gentlemen? is it to me? I swear it must not be; nay, trust me, in good faith it must not be; I cannot now command you, but I pray you for the respect you bare me, when you took me for your King, each man clap on his hat at my desire.

Mar.

We will, you are not found so mean a man, but that you may be cover'd as well as we, may you not?

Arb.

O not here, you may, but not I, for here is my Father in presence.

Mar.

Where?

Arb.

Why there: O the whole story would be a wilderness to lose thy self for ever: O pardon me dear Father for all the idle and unreverent words that I have spoke in idle moods to you: I am *Arbaces*, we all fellow-subjects, nor is the Queen *Panthea* now my Sister.

Bes.

Why if you remember fellow-subject *Arbaces*; I told you once she was not your sister: I, and she lookt nothing like you.

Arb.

I think you did, good Captain *Bessus*.

Bes.

Here will arise another question now amongst the Sword-men, whether I be to call him to account for beating me, now he is proved no King.

Enter Lygones.

Mar.

Sir here's Lygones, the agent for the Armenian State.

Arb.

Where is he? I know your business good Lygones.

Lyg.

We must have our King again, and will.

Arb.

I knew that was your business: you shall have your King again, and have him so again as never King was had, go one of you and bid *Bacurius* bring *Tigranes* hither; and bring the Lady with him, that *Panthea*, the Queen *Panthea* sent me word this [morning], was brave *Tigranes* mistress.

[*Ex. two Gent.*

Lyg.

'Tis *Spaconia*.

Arb.

I, I, *Spaconia*.

Lyg.

She is my Daughter.

Arb.

She is so: I could now tell any thing I never heard: your King shall go so home, as never man went.

Mar.

Shall he go on's head?

Arb.

He shall have chariots easier than air that I will have invented; and ne're think one shall pay any ransome, and thy self that art the messenger, shalt ride before him on a horse cut out of an intire Diamond, that shall be made to go with golden wheels, I know not how yet.

Lyg.

Why I shall be made for ever? they beli'd this King with us, and said he was unkind.

Arb.

And then thy Daughter, she shall have some strange thing, wee'l have the Kingdom sold utterly, and put into a toy which she shall wear about her carelesly some where or other. See the vertuous Queen; behold the humblest subject that you have kneel here before you.

Enter Panthea *And* 1 Gent.

Pan.

Why kneel you to me that am your Vassal?

Arb.

Grant me one request.

Pan.

Alas what can I grant you? what I can, I will.

Arb.

That you will please to marry me if I can prove it lawfull.

Pan.

Is that all? more willingly than I would draw this air.

Arb.

I'le kiss this hand in earnest.

2 Gent.

Sir, *Tigranes* is coming though he made it strange at first, to see the Princess any more.

Enter Tigranes *And* Spaconia.

Arb.

The Queen thou meanest, O my *Tigranes*. Pardon me, tread on my neck, I freely offer it, and if thou beest so given take revenge, for I have injur'd thee.

Tigr.

No, I forgive, and rejoyce more that you have found repentance, than I my liberty.

Arb.

Mayest thou be happy in thy fair choice, for thou art temperate.
You owe no ransom to the state, know that I have a thousand joyes
to tell you of, which yet I dare not utter till I pay my thanks
to Heaven for 'em: Will you go with me and help me? pray you do.

Tigr.

I will.

Arb.

Take then your fair one with you; and you Queen of goodness and
of us, O give me leave to take your arm in mine: come every one
that takes delight in goodness, help to sing loud thanks for me,
that I am prov'd no King.

Actus Quinti Scaena Prima.

Enter Mardonius, and Ligones.

Mar.

Sir, the King has seene your Commission, and beleeves it, and freely by this warrant gives you leave to visit Prince *Tigranes* your noble Master.

Lig.

I thanke his Grace, and kisse his hands.

Mar.

But is the maine of all your businesse
Ended in this?

Lig.

I have another, but a worse; I am asham'd, it is a businesse.--

Mar.

You serve a worthy person, and a stranger I am sure you are; you may imploy mee if you please, without your purse, such Officers should ever be their owne rewards.

Lig.

I am bound to your noblenesse.

Mar.

I may have neede of you, and then this curtesie,
If it be any, is not ill bestowed:
But may I civilly desire the rest?
I shall not be a hurter, if no helper.

Lig.

Sir, you shall know I have lost a foolish daughter,
And with her all my patience; pilferd away
By a meane Captaine of your Kings.

Mar.

Stay there Sir:
If he have reacht the noble worth of Captaine,
He may well claime a worthy gentlewoman,
Though shee were yours, and noble.

Lig.

I grant all that too: but this wretched fellow
Reaches no further then the emptie name,
That serves to feede him; were he valiant,
Or had but in him any noble nature,
That might hereafter promise him a good man;
My cares were something lighter, and my grave
A span yet from me.

Mar.

I confesse such fellowes
Be in all royall Campes, and have, and must be
To make the sinne of coward more detested
In the meane Souldier, that with such a foyle
Sets of much valour: By description
I should now guesse him to you. It was *Bessus*,
I dare almost with confidence pronounce it.

Lig.

Tis such a scurvy name as *Bessus*, and now I thinke tis hee.

Mar.

Captaine, doe you call him?
Beleeve me Sir, you have a miserie
Too mighty for your age: A pox upon him,
For that must be the end of all his service:
Your daughter was not mad Sir?

Lig.

No, would shee had beene,
The fault had had more credit: I would doe something.

Mar.

I would faine counsell you; but to what I know not:
Hee's so below a beating, that the women
Find him not worthy of their distaves; and
To hang him, were to cast away a rope,

Hee's such an ayrie thin unbodied coward,
That no revenge can catch him:
He tell you Sir, and tell you truth; this rascall
Feares neither God nor man, has beene so beaten:
Sufferance has made him wanscote; he has had
Since hee was first a slave, at least three hundred daggers
Set in his head, as little boyes doe new knives in hot meat;
Ther's not a rib in's bodie a my conscience,
That has not beene thrice broken with drie beating;
And now his sides looke like to wicker targets,
Everie way bended:
Children will shortly take him for a wall,
And set their stone-bowes in his forhead: is of so low a sence,
I cannot in a weeke imagine what should be done to him.

Lig.

Sure I have committed some great sinne,
That this strange fellow should be made my rod:
I would see him, but I shall have no patience:

Mar.

Tis no great matter if you have not, if a laming of him, or such a toy may doe you pleasure Sir, he has it for you, and Ile helpe you to him: tis no newes to him to have a leg broke, or a shoulder out, with being turnd ath' stones like a Tanzie: Draw not your sword, if you love it; for my conscience his head will break it: we use him ith' warres like a Ramme to shake a wall withall; here comes the verie person of him, doe as you shall find your temper I must leave you: but if you doe not breake him like a bisket, you are much too blame Sir. Ex. Mardo. Enter Bessus and Sword-men.

Lig.

Is your name Bessus?

Bes.

Men call me Captaine Bessus.

Lig.

Then Captaine **Bessus** you are a ranke rascall, without more exordiums, a durty frozen slave; and with the favour of your friends here, I will beate you.

2.

Pray use your pleasure Sir, you seem to be a gentleman.

Lig.

Thus Captaine **Bessus**, thus; thus twinge your nose, thus kicke you, and thus tread you.

Bess.

I doe beseech you yeeld your cause Sir quickly.

Lig.

Indeed I should have told you that first.

Bess.

I take it so.

1.

Captaine, a should indeed, he is mistaken:

Lig.

Sir you shall have it quickly, and more beating,
You have stolne away a Lady Captaine Coward,
And such a one.

Bes.

Hold, I beseech you, hold Sir,
I never yet stole any living thing
That had a tooth about it.

Lig.

Sir I know you dare lie
With none but Summer Whores upon my life Sir.

Bes.

My meanes and manners never could attempt
Above a hedge or hey-cocke.

Lig.

Sirra that quits not me, where is this Ladie,

Doe that you doe not use to doe, tell truth,
Or by my hand Ile beat your Captaines braines out.
Wash um, and put um in againe, that will I.

Bes.

There was a Ladie Sir, I must confesse
Once in my charge: the Prince *Tigranes* gave her
To my guard for her safetie, how I usd her
She may her selfe report, shee's with the Prince now:
I did but waite upon her like a Groome,
Which she will testifie I am sure: If not,
My braines are at your service when you please Sir,
And glad I have um for you?

Lig.

This is most likely, Sir I aske your pardon,
And am sorrie I was so intemperate.

Bes.

Well, I can aske no more, you would thinke it strange Now to have me beat you at first sight.

Lig.

Indeed I would but I know your goodnes can forget
Twentie beatings. You must forgive me.

Bes.

Yes, ther's my hand, goe where you will, I shall thinke

You a valiant fellow for all this.

Lig.

My daughter is a Whore,
I feele it now too sencible; yet I will see her,
Discharge my selfe of being Father to her,
And then backe to my Countrie, and there die;
Farewell Captaine.

Exit.

Bes.

Farewell Sir, farewell, commend me to the Gentlewoman I praia.

1.

How now Captaine, beare up man.

Bes.

Gentlemen ath' sword your hands once more, I have
Beene kickt againe, but the foolish fellow is penitent,
Has ask't me mercy, and my honor's safe.

2.

We knew that, or the foolish fellow had better a kick't
His Grandsire.
Confirme, confirme I pray.

1.

There be our hands againe.

2.

Now let him come, and say he was not sorry,
And he sleepes for it.

Bes.

Alas good ignorant old man, let him goe,
Let him goe, these courses will undoe him.

Exeunt.

Enter Ligones, and Bacurius.

Bac.

My Lord your authoritie is good, and I am glad it is so, for my consent would never hinder you from seeing your owne King. I am a Minister, but not a governour of this state; yonder is your King,
Ile leave you.

Exit.

Lig.

There he is indeed, *Enter Tig. and Spaco.*
And with him my disloyall childe.

Tig.

I doe perceive my fault so much, that yet
Me thinkes thou shouldst not have forgiven me.

Lig.

Health to your Maiestie.

Tig.

What? good Ligones, welcome; what businesse brought thee hether?

Lig.

Severall Businesses.
My publique businesse will appear by this:
I have a message to deliver, which
If it please you so to authorise, is
An embassage from the Armenian state,
Unto **Arbaces** for your libertie:
The offer's there set downe, please you to read it.

Tig.

There is no alteration happened
Since I came thence?

Lig.

None Sir, all is as it was.

Tig.

And all our friends are well.

Lig.

All verie well.

Spa.

Though I have done nothing but what was good,
I dare not see my Father: it was fault
Enough not to acquaint him with that good.

Lig.

Madam I should have scene you.

Spa.

O good Sir forgive me.

Lig.

Forgive you, why I am no kin to you, am I?

Spa.

Should it be measur'd by my meane deserts,
Indeed you are not.

Lig.

Thou couldst prate unhappily
Ere thou couldst goe, would thou couldst doe as well.
And how does your custome hold out here. *Spa*. Sir.

Lig.

Are you in private still, or how?

Spa.

What doe you meane?

Lig.

Doe you take money? are you come to sell sinne yet? perhaps I can helpe you to liberall Clients: or has not the King cast you off yet? O thou wild creature, whose best commendation is, that thou art a young Whore. I would thy Mother had liv'd to see this: or rather would I had dyed ere I had seene it: why did'st not make me acquainted when thou wert first resolv'd to be a Whore? I would have seene thy hot lust satisfied more privately. I would have kept a dancer, and a whole consort of Musitions in mine owne house, onely to fiddle thee. *Spa*. Sir I was never whore.

Lig.

If thou couldst not say so much for thy selfe thou shouldst be
Carted.

Tig.

Ligones I have read it, and like it,
You shall deliver it.

Lig.

Well Sir I will: but I have private busines with you.

Tig.

Speake, what ist?

Lig.

How has my age deserv'd so ill of you,
That you can picke no strumpets in the Land,
But out of my breed.

Tig.

Strumpets good ***Ligones***?

Lig.

Yes, and I wish to have you know, I scorne
To get a Whore for any Prince alive,
And yet scorne will not helpe me thinkes: My daughter
Might have beene spar'd, there were enough beside.

Tig.

May I not prosper, but Shee's innocent

As morning light for me, and I dare sweare
For all the world.

Lig.

Why is she with you then?
Can she waite on you better then your men,
Has she a gift in plucking off your stockings,
Can she make Cawdles well, or cut your Comes,
Why doe you keepe her with you? For your Queene
I know you doe contemne her, so should I
And every Subject else thinke much at it.

Tig.

Let um thinke much, but tis more firme then earth
Thou seest thy Queene there.

Lig.

Then have I made a faire hand, I cald her Whore,
If I shall speake now as her Father, I cannot chuse
But greatly rejoyce that she shall be a Queene: but if
I should speake to you as a Statesman shee were more fit
To be your Whore.

Tig.

Get you about your businesse to **Arbaces**,
Now you talke idlie.

Lig.

Yes Sir, I will goe.
And shall she be a Queene, she had more wit
Then her old Father when she ranne away:
Shall shee be a Queene, now by my troth tis fine,
Ile dance out of all measure at her wedding:
Shall I not Sir?

Tigr.

Yes marrie shalt thou.

Lig.

He make these witherd Kexes beare my bodie
Two houres together above ground.

Tigr.

Nay, goe, my businesse requires haste.

Lig.

Good God preserve you, you are an excellent King.

Spa.

Farewell good Father.

Lig.

Farewell sweete vertuous Daughter;

I never was so joyfull in my life,
That I remember: shall shee be a Queene?
Now I perceive a man may weepe for joy,
I had thought they had lied that said so.

Exit.

Tig.

Come my deare love.

Spa.

But you may see another
May alter that againe.

Tigr.

Urge it no more;
I have made up a new strong constancie,
Not to be shooke with eyes; I know I have
The passions of a man, but if I meete
With any subject that shall hold my eyes
More firmely then is fit; Ile thinke of thee,
and runne away from it: let that suffice.

Exeunt.

Enter Bacurius, and a servant.

Bac.

Three gentlemen without to speake with me?

Ser.

Yes Sir.

Bac.

Let them come in.

Ser.

They are enterd Sir already.

Enter Bessus, and Swordmen.

Bac.

Now fellowes, your busines, are these the Gentlemen.

Bess.

My Lord I have made bold to bring these Gentlemen my Friends ath' sword along with me.

Bac.

I am afraid youle fight then.

Bes.

My good Lord I will not, your Lordship is mistaken,
Feare not Lord.

Bac.

Sir I am sorrie fort.

Bes.

I can aske no more in honor, Gentlemen you heare my Lord is sorrie.

Bac.

Not that I have beaten you, but beaten one that will be beaten: one whose dull bodie will require launcing: As surfeits doe the diet, spring and full. Now to your swordmen, what come they for good Captaine Stock-fish?

Bes.

It seemes your Lordship has forgot my name.

Bac.

No, nor your nature neither, though they are things fitter I confesse for anything, then my remembrance, or anie honestmans, what shall these billets doe, be pilde up in my Wood-yard?

Bes.

Your Lordship holds your mirth still, God continue it: but for these Gentlemen they come.

Bac.

To sweare you are a Coward, spare your Booke, I doe beleeve it.

Bes.

Your Lordship still drawes wide, they come to vouch under their valiant hands, I am no Coward.

Bac.

That would be a shew indeed worth seeing: sirra be wise and take money for this motion, travell with it, and where the name of *Bessus* has been knowne, or a good Coward stirring, twill yeeld more then a tilting. This will prove more beneficiall to you, if you be thriftie, then your Captaineship, and more naturall; Men of most valiant hands is this true?

2.

It is so most renowned,
Tis somewhat strange.

1.

Lord, it is strange, yet true; wee have examined from your Lordships foote there to this mans head, the nature of the beatings; and we doe find his honour is come off cleane, and sufficient: This as our swords shall helpe us.

Bac.

You are much bound to you bilbow-men, I am glad you are straight again Captaine: twere good you would thinke some way to gratifie them, they have undergone a labour for you *Bessus*, would have puzzled *hercules*, with all his valour.

2.

Your Lordship must understand we are no men ath' Law, that take pay for our opinions: it is sufficient wee have cleer'd our friend.

Bac.

Yet here is something due, which I as toucht in conscience will discharge Captaine; Ile pay this rent for you.

Bess.

Spare your selfe my good Lord; my brave friends aime at nothing but the vertue.

Bac.

Thats but a cold discharge Sir for their paines.

2.

O Lord, my good Lord.

Bac.

Be not so modest, I will give you something.

Bes.

They shall dine with your Lordship, that's sufficient.

***Bac*.**

Something in hand the while; ye rogues, ye apple-squiers: doe you come hether with your botled valour, your windie frothe, to limit out my beatings.

***1*.**

I doe beseech your Lordship.

***2*.**

O good Lord.

***Bac*.**

Sfoote, what a many of beaten slaves are here? get me a cudgell sirra, and a tough one.

***2*.**

More of your foot, I doe beseech your Lordship.

***Bac*.**

You shall, you shall dog, and your fellow beagle.

***1*.**

A this side good my Lord.

Bac.

Off with your swords, for if you hurt my foote, Ile have you fleade you rascals.

1.

Mines off my Lord.

2.

I beseech your Lordship stay a little, my strap's tied to my codpiece point: Now when you please.

Bac.

Captaine, these are your valiant friends, you long for a little too?

Bess.

I am verie well, I humblie thanke your Lordship.

Bac.

Whats that in your pocket slave, my key you mungrell? thy buttocks cannot be so hard, out with't quicklie.

2.

Here tis Sir, a small piece of Artillerie, that a gentleman a deare friend of your Lordships sent me with to get it mended Sir; for it you marke, the nose is somewhat loose.

Bac.

A friend of mine you rascall, I was never wearier of doing nothing, then kicking these two foote-bals.

Ser.

Heres a good cudgell Sir.

Bac.

It comes too late; I am wearie, prethee doe thou beate um.

2.

My Lord this is foule play ifaith, to put a fresh man upon us; Men, are but men.

Bac.

That jest shall save your bones, up with your rotten regiment, and be gone; I had rather thresh, then be bound to kicke these raskals, till they cride hold: ***Bessus*** you may put your hand to them now, and then you are quit. Farewell, as you like this, pray visit mee againe, twill keepe me in good breath.

2.

Has a divellish hard foote, I never felt the like.

1.

Nor I, and yet Ime sure I ha felt a hundred.

2.

If he kicke thus ith dog-daies, he will be drie founderd: what cure now Captaine, besides oyle of bayes?

Bess.

Why well enough I warrant you, you can goe.

2.

Yes, God be thanked; but I feele a shrewd ach, sure he has sprang my huckle bone.

1.

I ha lost a haunch.

Bess.

A little butter friend, a little butter; butter and parselie is a soveraigne matter: ***probatum est***.

1.

Captaine, we must request your hands now to our honours.

Bess.

Yes marrie shall ye, and then let all the world come, we are valiant to our selves, and theres an end.

1.

Nay, then we must be valiant; O my ribbes.

2.

O my small guts, a plague upon these sharpe toe'd shooes, they are murderers.

Exeunt.

Enter Arbaces with his Sword drawne.

Arb.

It is resolv'd, I bore it whilst I could,
I can no more, Hell open all thy gates,
And I will thorough them; if they be shut,
Ile batter um, but I will find the place
Where the most damn'd have dwelling; ere I end,
Amongst them all they shall not have a sinne,
But I may call it mine: I must beginne
With murder of my friend, and so goe on
To an incestuous ravishing, and end
My life and sinnes with a forbidden blow
Upon my selfe.

Enter Mardonius.

Mardo.

What Tragedie is here?
That hand was never wont to draw a Sword,

A King, and No King

But it cride dead to something:

Arb.

Mar. have you bid *Gobrius* come?

Mar.

How doe you Sir?

Arb.

Well, is he comming?

Mar.

Why Sir are you thus?
Why does your hand proclaime a lawlesse warre
Against your selfe?

Arb.

Thou answerest me one question with another,
Is *Gobrius* comming?

Mar.

Sir he is. *Arb*. Tis well.

Mar.

I can forbeare your questions then, be gone
Sir, I have markt.

Arb.

Marke lesse, it troubles you and me.

Mar.

You are more variable then you were.

Arb.

It may be so.

Mar.

To day no Hermit could be humblier
Then you were to us all.

Arb.

And what of this?

Mar.

And now you take new rage into your eies,
As you would looke us all out of the Land.

Arb.

I doe confesse it, will that satisfie,
I prethee get thee gone.

Mar.

Sir I will speake.

Arb.

Will ye?

Mar.

It is my dutie,
I feare you will kill your selfe: I am a subject,
And you shall doe me wrong in't: tis my cause,
And I may speake.

Arb.

Thou art not traind in sinne,
It seemes *Mardonius*: kill my selfe, by heaven
I will not doe it yet; and when I will,
Ile tell thee then: I shall be such a creature,
That thou wilt give me leave without a word.
There is a method in mans wickednesse,
It growes up by degrees; I am not come
So high as killing of my selfe, there are
A hundred thousand sinnes twixt me and it,
Which I must doe, I shall come toot at last;
But take my oath not now, be satisfied,

And get thee hence.

Mar.

I am sorrie tis so ill.

Arb.

Be sorrie then,
True sorrow is alone, grieve by thy selfe.

Mar.

I pray you let mee see your sword put up
Before I goe; Ile leave you then.

Arb.

Why so?
What follie is this in thee? is it not
As apt to mischiefe as it was before?
Can I not reach it thinkest thou? these are toyes
For children to be pleas'd with, and not men;
Now I am safe you thinke: I would the booke
Of Fate were here, my sword is not so sure,
But I should get it out, and mangle that
That all the destinies should quite forget
Their fix't decrees, and hast to make us new
Farre other Fortunes mine could not be worse,
Wilt thou now leave me?

Mar.

God put into your bosome temperate thoughts,
He leave you though I feare.

Exit.

Arb.

Goe, thou art honest,
Why should the hastie errors of my youth
Be so unpardonable, to draw a sinne
Helpelesse upon me?

Enter Gobrius.

Gob.

There is the King, now it is ripe.

Arb.

Draw neere thou guiltie man,
That are the author of the loathedst crime
Five ages have brought forth, and heare me speake
Curses incurable, and all the evils
Mans bodie or his spirit can receive
Be with thee.

Gob.

Why Sir doe you curse me thus?

Arb.

Why doe I curse thee, if there be a man
Subtill in curses, that exceedes the rest,
His worst wish on thee. Thou hast broke my hart.

Gob.

How Sir? Have I preserv'd you from a childe,
From all the arrowes, malice or ambition
Could shoot at you, and have I this for pay?

Arb.

Tis true thou didst preserve me, and in that
Wert crueller then hardned murderers
Of infants and their mothers; thou didst save me
Onely till thou hadst studdied out a way
How to destroy me cunningly thy selfe:
This was a curious way of torturing.

Gob.

What doe you meane?

Arb.

Thou knowst the evils thou hast done to me,
Dost thou remember all those witching letters
Thou sentst unto me to **Armenia**,
Fild with the praise of my beloved Sister,
Where thou extolst her beautie; what had I
To doe with that, what could her beautie be

To me, and thou didst write how well shee lov'd me,
Doest thou remember this: so that I doated
Something before I saw her.

Gob.

This is true.

Arb.

Is it, and I when I was returnd thou knowst
Thou didst pursue it, till thou woundst mee into
Such a strange, and unbeleev'd affection,
As good men cannot thinke on.

Gob.

This I grant, I thinke I was the cause.

Arb.

Wert thou? Nay more, I thinke thou meantst it.

Gob.

Sir I hate a lie.
As I love God and honestie, I did:
It was my meaning.

Arb.

Be thine owne sad Judge,
A further condemnation will not need:

Prepare thy selfe to die.

Gob.

Why Sir to die?

Arb.

Why wouldst thou live, was ever yet offender
So impudent, that had a thought of mercy
After confession of a crime like this?
Get out I cannot, where thou hurlst me in,
But I can take revenge, that's all the sweetnesse
Left for me.

Gob.

Now is the time, heare me but speake.

Arb.

No, yet I will be farre more mercifull
Then thou wert to me; thou didst steale into me,
And never gavest me warning: so much time
As I give thee now, had prevented thee
For ever. Notwithstanding all thy sinnes,
If thou hast hope, that there is yet a prayer
To save thee, turne, and speake it to your selfe.

Gob.

Sir, you shall know your sinnes before you doe um
If you kill me.

Arb.

I will not stay then.

Gob.

Know you kill your Father.

Arb.

How?

Gob.

You kill your Father.

Arb.

My Father? though I know it for a lie
Made out of feare to save thy stained life:
The verie reverence of the word comes crosse me,
And ties mine arme downe.

Gob.

I will tell you that shall heighten you againe, I am thy
Father, I charge thee heare me.

Arb.

If it should be so,
As tis most false, and that I should be found
A bastard issue, the dispised fruite

Of lawlesse lust, I should no more admire
All my wilde passions: but another truth
Shall be wrung from thee: If I could come by
The spirit of paine, it should be powr'd on thee,
Till thou allowest thy selfe more full of lies
Then he that teaches thee.

Enter Arane.

Arane.

Turne thee about,
I come to speake to thee thou wicked man,
Heare me thou Tyrant.

Arb.

I will turne to thee,
Heare me thou Strumpet: I have blotted out
The name of mother, as thou hast thy shame.

Ara.

My shame, thou hast lesse shame then anything:
Why dost thou keepe my daughter in a prison?
Why dost thou call her Sister, and doe this?

Arb.

Cease thou strange impudence, and answere quickly,
If thou contemn'st me, this will aske an answere,
And have it.

Ara.

Helpe me gentle *Gobrius*.

Arb.

Guilt dare not helpe guilt, though they grow together
In doing ill, yet at the punishment
They sever, and each flies the noyse of other,
Thinke not of helpe, answere.

Ara.

I will, to what?

Arb.

To such a thing as if it be a truth,
Thinke what a creature thou hast made thy selfe,
That didst not shame to doe, what I must blush
Onely to aske thee: tell me who I am,
Whose sonne I am, without all circumstance;
Be thou as hastie, as my Sword will be
If thou refusest.

Ara.

Why you are his sonne.

Arb.

His sonne?
Sweare, sweare, thou worse then woman damn'd.

Ara.

By all thats good you are.

Arb.

Then art thou all that ever was knowne bad. Now is
The cause of all my strange misfortunes come to light:
What reverence expects thou from a childe
To bring forth which thou hast offended Heaven,
Thy husband and the Land: Adulterous witch
I know now why thou wouldst have poyson'd me,
I was thy lust which thou wouldst have forgot:
Thou wicked mother of my sinnes, and me,
Shew me the way to the inheritance
I have by thee: which is a spacious world
Of impious acts, that I may soone possesse it:
Plagues rott thee, as thou liv'st, and such diseases
As use to pay lust, recompence thy deed.

Gob.

You doe not know why you curse thus.

Arb.

Too well:
You are a paire of Vipers, and behold
The Serpent you have got; there is no beast
But if he knew, it has a pedigree
As brave as mine, for they have more discents,
And I am every way as beastly got,
As farre without the compasse of a law,

As they.

Ara.

You spend your rage, and words in vaine,
And raile upon a guesse: heare us a little.

Arb.

No I will never heare, but talke away
My breath, and die.

Gob.

Why but you are no Bastard.

Arb.

Howe's that?

Ara.

Nor childe of mine.

Arb.

Still you goe on in wonders to me.

Gob.

Pray be more patient, I may bring comfort to you.

Arb.

    I will kneele,
And heare with the obedience of a childe;
Good Father speake, I doe acknowledge you,
So you bring comfort.

Gob.

    First know our last King your supposed Father
Was olde and feeble when he marryed her,
And almost all the Land as shee past hope
Of issue from him.

Arb.

    Therefore shee tooke leave
To play the whoore, because the King was old:
Is this the comfort?

Ara.

    What will you find out
To give me satisfaction, when you find
How you have injur'd me: let fire consume mee,
If ever I were whore.

Gob.

    Forbeare these starts,
Or I will leave you wedded to despaire,
As you are now: if you can find a temper,
My breath shall be a pleasant westerne wind,

That cooles, and blasts not.

Arb.

Bring it out good Father,
He lie, artd listen here as reverentlie
As to an Angell: If I breathe too loude,
Tell me; for I would be as still as night.

Gob.

Our King I say was old, and this our Queene
Desired to bring an heire; but yet her husband
Shee thought was past it, and to be dishonest
I thinke shee would not; if shee would have beene,
The truth is, shee was watcht so narrowlie,
And had so slender opportunitie,
Shee hardly could have beene: But yet her cunning
Found out this way; shee fain'd her selfe with child,
And postes were sent in haste throughout the Land,
And God was humbly thankt in every Church,
That so had blest the Queen, and prayers were made
For her safe going, and deliverie:
Shee fain'd now to grow bigger, and perceiv'd
This hope of issue made her feard, and brought
A farre more large respect from everie man.
And saw her power increase, and was resolv'd,
Since shee believ'd shee could not have't indeede;
At least shee would be thought to have a child.

Arb.

Doe I not heare it well: nay, I will make

No noise at all; but pray you to the point,
Quicke as you can.

Gob.

Now when the time was full,
Shee should be brought abed; I had a sonne
Borne, which was you: This the Queene hearing of,
Mov'd me to let her have you, and such reasons
Shee shewed me, as shee knew would tie
My secresie: shee sware you should be King;
And to be short, I did deliver you
Unto her, and pretended you were dead;
And in mine owne house kept a Funerall,
And had an emptie coffin put in earth:
That night the Queene fain'd hastilie to labour,
And by a paire of women of her owne,
Which shee had charm'd, shee made the world believe
Shee was deliver'd of you: you grew up
As the Kings sonne, till you were six yeere olde;
Then did the King die, and did leave to me
Protection of the Realme; and contrarie
To his owne expectation, left this Queene
Truly with Childe indeed of the faire Princesse
Panthea: Then shee could have torne her heire,
And did alone to me yet durst not speake
In publike; for shee knew shee should be found
A Traytor, and her talke would have beene thought
Madnesse or any thing rather then truth:
This was the onely cause why shee did seeke
To poyson you, and I to keepe you safe:
And this the reason why I sought to kindle
Some sparke of love in you to faire *Panthea*,

That shee might get part of her right agen.

Arb.

And have you made an end now, is this all?
If not, I will be still till I am aged,
Till all my heires are silver.

Gob.

This is all.

Arb.

And is it true say you Maddam?

Ara.

Yes, God knowes it is most true.

Arb.

Panthea then is not my Sister.

Gob.

No.

Arb.

But can you prove this?

[*Gob*.]

If you will give consent: else who dare goe about it.

Arb.

Give consent?
Why I will have them all that know it rackt
To get this from um: All that waites without
Come in, what ere you be come in, and be
Partakers of my Joy: O you are welcome.

Ent. Mar: Bessus, and others.

Mardonius the best newes, nay, draw no neerer
They all shall heare it: I am found no King.

Mar.

Is that so good newes?

Art.

Yes, the happiest newes that ere was heard.

Mar.

Indeed twere well for you,
If you might be a little lesse obey'd.

Arb.

On, call the Queene.

Mar.

Why she is there.

Arb.

The Queene *Mardonius*, *Panthea* is the Queene,
And I am plaine *Arbaces*, goe some one,
She is in *Gobrius* house; since I saw you
There are a thousand things delivered to me
You little dreame of.

Mar.

So it should seeme: My Lord,
What furi's this.

Gob.

Beleeve me tis no fury,
All that he sayes is truth.

Mar.

Tis verie strange.

Arb.

Why doe you keepe your hats off Gentlemen,
Is it to me? in good faith it must not be:
I cannot now command you, but I pray you
For the respect you bare me, when you tooke
Me for your King, each man clap on his hat at my desire.

Mar.

We will: but you are not found
So meane a man, but that you may be cover'd
As well as we, may you not?

Arb.

O not here,
You may, but not I, for here is my Father in presence.

Mar.

Where?

Arb.

Why there: O the whole storie
Would be a wildernesse to loose thy selfe
For ever; O pardon me deare Father,
For all the idle, and unreverent words
That I have spoke in idle moodes to you:
I am *Arbaces*, we all fellow subjects,
Nor is the Queene *Panthea* now my Sister.

Bes.

Why if you remember fellow subject *Arbaces*, I tolde you once
she was not your sister, I say she look't nothing like you.

Arb.

I thinke you did good Captaine *Bessus*.

Bes.

Here will arise another question now amongst the Swordmen,
whether I be to call him to account for beating me, now he's
prov'd no King.

Enter Ligones.

Ma.

Sir, heres *Ligones*
The Agent for the Armenian King.

Arb.

Where is he, I know your businesse good *Ligones*.

Lig.

We must have our King againe, and will.

Arb.

I knew that was your businesse, you shall have
You King againe, and have him so againe
As never King was had. Goe one of you
And bid *Bacurius* bring *Tigranes* hither,
And bring the Ladie with him, that *Panthea*
The Queene *Panthea* sent me word this morning
Was brave *Tigranes* mistresse.

Lig.

Tis *Spaconia*.

Arb.

I, I, *Spaconia*.

Lig.

She is my daughter.

Arb.

Shee is so, I could now tell any thing
I never heard; your King shall goe so home
As never man went.

Mar.

Shall he goe on's head?

Arb.

He shall have Chariots easier than ayre
That I will have invented; and nere thinke
He shall pay any ransome; and thy selfe
That art the Messenger shall ride before him
On a Horse cut out of an entire Diamond,
That shall be made to goe with golden wheeles,
I know not how yet.

Lig.

Why I shall be made
For ever, they belied this King with us
And sayd he was unkind.

Arb.

And then thy daughter,
She shall have some strange thinke, wele have the Kingdome
Sold utterly, and put into a toy.
Which she shall weare about her carelesly
Some where or other.
See the vertuous Queene.

    Enter Pan.

Behold the humblest subject that you have
Kneele here before you. *Pan*. Why kneele you
To me that am your vassall?

Arb.

Grant me one request.

Pan.

Alas, what can I grant you?
What I can I will.

Arb.

That you will please to marry me,

If I can prove it lawfull.

Pan.

Is that all?
More willingly, then I would draw this ayre.

Arb.

Ile kisse this hand in earnest.

Mar.

Sir, *Tigranes* is comming though he made it strange
To see the Princesse any more.

Arb.

The Queene,

   Enter Tig. and Spa.

Thou meanest: O my Tigranes pardon me,
Tread on my necke I freely offer it,
And if thou beest so given; take revenge,
For I have injur'd thee.

Tig.

No, I forgive,
And rejoice more that you have found repentance,
Then I my libertie.

Arb.

Maist thou be happie
In thy faire choice; for thou art temperate:
You owe no ransome to the state, know that;
I have a thousand joyes to tell you of,
Which yet I dare not utter, till I pay
My thankes to Heaven for um: will you goe
With me, and helpe me; pray you doe.

Tig.

I will.

Arb.

Take then your faire one with you and your Queene
Of goodnesse, and of us; O give me leave
To take your arme in mine: Come every one
That takes delight in goodnesse, helpe to sing
Loude thankes for me, that I am prov'd no King.

www.bookjungle.com *email: sales@bookjungle.com fax: 630-214-0564 mail: Book Jungle PO Box 2226 Champaign, IL 61825*

The Codes Of Hammurabi And Moses
W. W. Davies

QTY

The discovery of the Hammurabi Code is one of the greatest achievements of archaeology, and is of paramount interest, not only to the student of the Bible, but also to all those interested in ancient history...

Religion   **ISBN:** *1-59462-338-4*   Pages:132
MSRP *$12.95*

The Theory of Moral Sentiments
Adam Smith

QTY

This work from 1749. contains original theories of conscience amd moral judgment and it is the foundation for systemof morals.

Philosophy   **ISBN:** *1-59462-777-0*   Pages:536
MSRP *$19.95*

Jessica's First Prayer
Hesba Stretton

QTY

In a screened and secluded corner of one of the many railway-bridges which span the streets of London there could be seen a few years ago, from five o'clock every morning until half past eight, a tidily set-out coffee-stall, consisting of a trestle and board, upon which stood two large tin cans, with a small fire of charcoal burning under each so as to keep the coffee boiling during the early hours of the morning when the work-people were thronging into the city on their way to their daily toil...

Childrens   **ISBN:** *1-59462-373-2*   Pages:84
MSRP *$9.95*

My Life and Work
Henry Ford

QTY

Henry Ford revolutionized the world with his implementation of mass production for the Model T automobile. Gain valuable business insight into his life and work with his own auto-biography... "We have only started on our development of our country we have not as yet, with all our talk of wonderful progress, done more than scratch the surface. The progress has been wonderful enough but..."

Biographies/   **ISBN:** *1-59462-198-5*   Pages:300
MSRP *$21.95*

www.bookjungle.com email: sales@bookjungle.com fax: 630-214-0564 mail: Book Jungle PO Box 2226 Champaign, IL 61825

The Art of Cross-Examination
Francis Wellman

QTY

I presume it is the experience of every author, after his first book is published upon an important subject, to be almost overwhelmed with a wealth of ideas and illustrations which could readily have been included in his book, and which to his own mind, at least, seem to make a second edition inevitable. Such certainly was the case with me; and when the first edition had reached its sixth impression in five months, I rejoiced to learn that it seemed to my publishers that the book had met with a sufficiently favorable reception to justify a second and considerably enlarged edition. ...

Reference   ISBN: *1-59462-647-2*   Pages:412 MSRP *$19.95*

On the Duty of Civil Disobedience
Henry David Thoreau

QTY

Thoreau wrote his famous essay, On the Duty of Civil Disobedience, as a protest against an unjust but popular war and the immoral but popular institution of slave-owning. He did more than write—he declined to pay his taxes, and was hauled off to gaol in consequence. Who can say how much this refusal of his hastened the end of the war and of slavery?

Law   ISBN: *1-59462-747-9*   Pages:48 MSRP *$7.45*

Dream Psychology Psychoanalysis for Beginners
Sigmund Freud

QTY

Sigmund Freud, born Sigismund Schlomo Freud (May 6, 1856 - September 23, 1939), was a Jewish-Austrian neurologist and psychiatrist who co-founded the psychoanalytic school of psychology. Freud is best known for his theories of the unconscious mind, especially involving the mechanism of repression; his redefinition of sexual desire as mobile and directed towards a wide variety of objects; and his therapeutic techniques, especially his understanding of transference in the therapeutic relationship and the presumed value of dreams as sources of insight into unconscious desires.

Psychology   ISBN: *1-59462-905-6*   Pages:196 MSRP *$15.45*

The Miracle of Right Thought
Orison Swett Marden

QTY

Believe with all of your heart that you will do what you were made to do. When the mind has once formed the habit of holding cheerful, happy, prosperous pictures, it will not be easy to form the opposite habit. It does not matter how improbable or how far away this realization may see, or how dark the prospects may be, if we visualize them as best we can, as vividly as possible, hold tenaciously to them and vigorously struggle to attain them, they will gradually become actualized, realized in the life. But a desire, a longing without endeavor, a yearning abandoned or held indifferently will vanish without realization.

Self Help   ISBN: *1-59462-644-8*   Pages:360 MSRP *$25.45*

www.bookjungle.com email: sales@bookjungle.com fax: 630-214-0564 mail: Book Jungle PO Box 2226 Champaign, IL 61825

QTY

☐ **The Rosicrucian Cosmo-Conception Mystic Christianity** by *Max Heindel* ISBN: *1-59462-188-8* **$38.95**
The Rosicrucian Cosmo-conception is not dogmatic, neither does it appeal to any other authority than the reason of the student. It is; not controversial, but is; sent forth in the, hope that it may help to clear... *New Age/Religion Pages 646*

☐ **Abandonment To Divine Providence** by *Jean-Pierre de Caussade* ISBN: *1-59462-228-0* **$25.95**
"The Rev. Jean Pierre de Caussade was one of the most remarkable spiritual writers of the Society of Jesus in France in the 18th Century. His death took place at Toulouse in 1751. His works have gone through many editions and have been republished... *Inspirational/Religion Pages 400*

☐ **Mental Chemistry** by *Charles Haanel* ISBN: *1-59462-192-6* **$23.95**
Mental Chemistry allows the change of material conditions by combining and appropriately utilizing the power of the mind. Much like applied chemistry creates something new and unique out of careful combinations of chemicals the mastery of mental chemistry... *New Age Pages 354*

☐ **The Letters of Robert Browning and Elizabeth Barret Barrett 1845-1846 vol II** ISBN: *1-59462-193-4* **$35.95**
by *Robert Browning* and *Elizabeth Barrett* *Biographies Pages 596*

☐ **Gleanings In Genesis (volume I)** by *Arthur W. Pink* ISBN: *1-59462-130-6* **$27.45**
Appropriately has Genesis been termed "the seed plot of the Bible" for in it we have, in germ form, almost all of the great doctrines which are afterwards fully developed in the books of Scripture which follow... *Religion/Inspirational Pages 420*

☐ **The Master Key** by *L. W. de Laurence* ISBN: *1-59462-001-6* **$30.95**
In no branch of human knowledge has there been a more lively increase of the spirit of research during the past few years than in the study of Psychology, Concentration and Mental Discipline. The requests for authentic lessons in Thought Control, Mental Discipline and... *New Age/Business Pages 422*

☐ **The Lesser Key Of Solomon Goetia** by *L. W. de Laurence* ISBN: *1-59462-092-X* **$9.95**
This translation of the first book of the "Lernegton" which is now for the first time made accessible to students of Talismanic Magic was done, after careful collation and edition, from numerous Ancient Manuscripts in Hebrew, Latin, and French... *New Age/Occult Pages 92*

☐ **Rubaiyat Of Omar Khayyam** by *Edward Fitzgerald* ISBN:*1-59462-332-5* **$13.95**
Edward Fitzgerald, whom the world has already learned, in spite of his own efforts to remain within the shadow of anonymity, to look upon as one of the rarest poets of the century, was born at Bredfield, in Suffolk, on the 31st of March, 1809. He was the third son of John Purcell... *Music Pages 172*

☐ **Ancient Law** by *Henry Maine* ISBN: *1-59462-128-4* **$29.95**
The chief object of the following pages is to indicate some of the earliest ideas of mankind, as they are reflected in Ancient Law, and to point out the relation of those ideas to modern thought. *Religiom/History Pages 452*

☐ **Far-Away Stories** by *William J. Locke* ISBN: *1-59462-129-2* **$19.45**
"Good wine needs no bush, but a collection of mixed vintages does. And this book is just such a collection. Some of the stories I do not want to remain buried for ever in the museum files of dead magazine-numbers an author's not unpardonable vanity..." *Fiction Pages 272*

☐ **Life of David Crockett** by *David Crockett* ISBN: *1-59462-250-7* **$27.45**
"Colonel David Crockett was one of the most remarkable men of the times in which he lived. Born in humble life, but gifted with a strong will, an indomitable courage, and unremitting perseverance... *Biographies/New Age Pages 424*

☐ **Lip-Reading** by *Edward Nitchie* ISBN: *1-59462-206-X* **$25.95**
Edward B. Nitchie, founder of the New York School for the Hard of Hearing, now the Nitchie School of Lip-Reading, Inc, wrote "LIP-READING Principles and Practice". The development and perfecting of this meritorious work on lip-reading was an undertaking... *How-to Pages 400*

☐ **A Handbook of Suggestive Therapeutics, Applied Hypnotism, Psychic Science** ISBN: *1-59462-214-0* **$24.95**
by *Henry Munro* *Health/New Age/Health/Self-help Pages 376*

☐ **A Doll's House: and Two Other Plays** by *Henrik Ibsen* ISBN: *1-59462-112-8* **$19.95**
Henrik Ibsen created this classic when in revolutionary 1848 Rome. Introducing some striking concepts in playwriting for the realist genre, this play has been studied the world over. *Fiction/Classics/Plays 308*

☐ **The Light of Asia** by *sir Edwin Arnold* ISBN: *1-59462-204-3* **$13.95**
In this poetic masterpiece, Edwin Arnold describes the life and teachings of Buddha. The man who was to become known as Buddha to the world was born as Prince Gautama of India but he rejected the worldly riches and abandoned the reigns of power when... *Religion/History/Biographies Pages 170*

☐ **The Complete Works of Guy de Maupassant** by *Guy de Maupassant* ISBN: *1-59462-157-8* **$16.95**
"For days and days, nights and nights, I had dreamed of that first kiss which was to consecrate our engagement, and I knew not on what spot I should put my lips..." *Fiction/Classics Pages 240*

☐ **The Art of Cross-Examination** by *Francis L. Wellman* ISBN: *1-59462-309-0* **$26.95**
Written by a renowned trial lawyer, Wellman imparts his experience and uses case studies to explain how to use psychology to extract desired information through questioning. *How-to/Science/Reference Pages 408*

☐ **Answered or Unanswered?** by *Louisa Vaughan* ISBN: *1-59462-248-5* **$10.95**
Miracles of Faith in China *Religion Pages 112*

☐ **The Edinburgh Lectures on Mental Science (1909)** by *Thomas* ISBN: *1-59462-008-3* **$11.95**
This book contains the substance of a course of lectures recently given by the writer in the Queen Street Hall, Edinburgh. Its purpose is to indicate the Natural Principles governing the relation between Mental Action and Material Conditions... *New Age/Psychology Pages 148*

☐ **Ayesha** by *H. Rider Haggard* ISBN: *1-59462-301-5* **$24.95**
Verily and indeed it is the unexpected that happens! Probably if there was one person upon the earth from whom the Editor of this, and of a certain previous history, did not expect to hear again... *Classics Pages 380*

☐ **Ayala's Angel** by *Anthony Trollope* ISBN: *1-59462-352-X* **$29.95**
The two girls were both pretty, but Lucy who was twenty-one who supposed to be simple and comparatively unattractive, whereas Ayala was credited, as her Bombwhat romantic name might show, with poetic charm and a taste for romance. Ayala when her father died was nineteen... *Fiction Pages 484*

☐ **The American Commonwealth** by *James Bryce* ISBN: *1-59462-286-8* **$34.45**
An interpretation of American democratic political theory. It examines political mechanics and society from the perspective of Scotsman James Bryce *Politics Pages 572*

☐ **Stories of the Pilgrims** by *Margaret P. Pumphrey* ISBN: *1-59462-116-0* **$17.95**
This book explores pilgrims religious oppression in England as well as their escape to Holland and eventual crossing to America on the Mayflower, and their early days in New England... *History Pages 268*

www.bookjungle.com email: sales@bookjungle.com fax: 630-214-0564 mail: Book Jungle PO Box 2226 Champaign, IL 61825

QTY

The Fasting Cure by *Sinclair Upton* ISBN: *1-59462-222-1* **$13.95**
In the Cosmopolitan Magazine for May, 1910, and in the Contemporary Review (London) for April, 1910, I published an article dealing with my experiences in fasting. I have written a great many magazine articles, but never one which attracted so much attention... *New Age/Self Help/Health Pages 164*

Hebrew Astrology by *Sepharial* ISBN: *1-59462-308-2* **$13.45**
In these days of advanced thinking it is a matter of common observation that we have left many of the old landmarks behind and that we are now pressing forward to greater heights and to a wider horizon than that which represented the mind-content of our progenitors... *Astrology Pages 144*

Thought Vibration or The Law of Attraction in the Thought World ISBN: *1-59462-127-6* **$12.95**
by *William Walker Atkinson* *Psychology/Religion Pages 144*

Optimism by *Helen Keller* ISBN: *1-59462-108-X* **$15.95**
Helen Keller was blind, deaf, and mute since 19 months old, yet famously learned how to overcome these handicaps, communicate with the world, and spread her lectures promoting optimism. An inspiring read for everyone... *Biographies/Inspirational Pages 84*

Sara Crewe by *Frances Burnett* ISBN: *1-59462-360-0* **$9.45**
In the first place, Miss Minchin lived in London. Her home was a large, dull, tall one, in a large, dull square, where all the houses were alike, and all the sparrows were alike, and where all the door-knockers made the same heavy sound... *Childrens/Classic Pages 88*

The Autobiography of Benjamin Franklin by *Benjamin Franklin* ISBN: *1-59462-135-7* **$24.95**
The Autobiography of Benjamin Franklin has probably been more extensively read than any other American historical work, and no other book of its kind has had such ups and downs of fortune. Franklin lived for many years in England, where he was agent... *Biographies/History Pages 332*

Name	
Email	
Telephone	
Address	
City, State ZIP	

☐ Credit Card   ☐ Check / Money Order

Credit Card Number	
Expiration Date	
Signature	

Please Mail to: Book Jungle
                   PO Box 2226
                   Champaign, IL 61825
or Fax to: 630-214-0564

ORDERING INFORMATION

web: *www.bookjungle.com*
email: *sales@bookjungle.com*
fax: *630-214-0564*
mail: *Book Jungle PO Box 2226 Champaign, IL 61825*
or PayPal *to sales@bookjungle.com*

Please contact us for bulk discounts

DIRECT-ORDER TERMS

**20% Discount if You Order
Two or More Books**
Free Domestic Shipping!
Accepted: Master Card, Visa,
Discover, American Express

www.ingramcontent.com/pod-product-compliance
Lightning Source LLC
Chambersburg PA
CBHW080240170426
43192CB00014BA/2513